A Reluctant Democrat

Glenmuick House
The house was designed by Sir Samuel Morton Peto in 1870 it was demolished in 1948 having fallen into disrepair during the Second World War

A RELUCTANT ARISTOCRAT

Assorted Memories of my Unconventional Life

GUY MACKENZIE

"Where ignorance is bliss, 'tis folly to be wise."
Thomas Gray

The right of Guy Mackenzie to be identified as the author of this work has been asserted by him in accordance with the Copyright, Design and Patents Act 1988.

All rights reserved. No part of this publication may be reproduced, stored in a retrieval system, or transmitted in any form or by any means, electronic, mechanical, photocopying, recording or otherwise without the prior permission of both the copyright owner and the publisher.

A Reluctant Aristocrat
©Guy Mackenzie
First published 2023
Edited, Designed & Typeset by: Toni Carver
Cover Design ©Sheila Moxley
Printed & Published by
The St Ives Printing & Publishing Company
High Street, St Ives, Cornwall TR26 1RS, UK
Telephone 01736 795813
www.stivesnews.co.uk

ISBN: 978-1-7398890-4-3

Foreword

POMP AND CIRCUMSTANCE, banquets and balls, might be assumed conventional fare in the life of Scottish aristocrat Sir James William Guy Mackenzie, 5th Baronet of Glenmuick. But, a tad 'reluctant' about that life-style his unconventional life saw him take no predestined path, although he remains proud of his family's achievements and his heritage. While he might, at times, have been on the edge of high class scandal and rubbed shoulders with his aristocratic peers he's happier behind his drum kit or interviewing one of his guitar heroes. The real 'aristocracy' for Guy is that of Rock 'n' Roll after being present at the now legendary Beatles' concert at Stowe School in Buckinghamshire on April 4th 1963. It might not be 'unconventional' for people to collect guitars but it is certainly most unusual to collect these wondrous 'axes' if you don't even play them!

Most of us '60s kids had a longing for America. Cultural influence came with television and Rock 'n' Roll in the mid-1950s, not to be diluted until December 1963 when The Beatles told the Yanks *I Wanna Hold your Hand* and America braced itself for the 'British Invasion'. We wanted to cruise down past *77 Sunset Strip* comb our hair, or flipping it, like Edd Byrnes' character Kookie in the series, then get our kicks on *Route 66*. Perhaps, then, it's not all that surprising that the unconventional heir to a Scottish baronetcy should be attracted to America, all things 'hair' (wigs not exempted!) and – the road. It was pretty conventional to dream of that mythical road trip along the legendary Route 66 but pretty unconventional to actually do it, selling hair products as you went. Guy did this, kicks and all!

Guy's memoir takes us from Ballater on Royal Deeside, to Calgary on the Isle of Mull through adventures in London, across America eventually to Cornwall where he became a property developer, a local councillor and still lives today. Remarkably, in assisting Guy with his book we found that at different times and for different reasons we had both frequented the same locations in Scotland and Cornwall. I spent several good holidays on the sacred Isle of Iona, sea kayaking around Mull and reconnected with my love of Scottish folk music at Calgary and in Tobermory.

I knew the often gnarly 'scene' around the derelict cottages Guy developed at Treen having been a sometime regular at Gurnard's Head Hotel from the mid-'60s. The pub lies in the heart of Cornwall's main sea-cliff climbing area and while climbers often come across naked couples 'in flagrante delicto' on remote cliff tops I have yet to experience a performance as graphic a Guy did on the climbers' bouldering (and nudist beach) of Pedn Vounder.

Toni Carver
Editor, *The St Ives Times & Echo*
July 2023

Acknowledgements

A GREAT MANY people have contributed in numerous ways to the assorted recollections of my unconventional life appearing in this memoir.

Carol & Danny Mutimer who did so much for our family when my mother lived in Norfolk. Paul Day the co-author of the inspirational *Ultimate Guitar Book* who was a source of advice and guitars(!) for many years and who helped me unearth my Supersound collection, the UK's first solid electric guitars. Lars Mullen, guitar journalist, who filmed most of my YouTube videos. Norman 'Shadow Cat' who helped, advised me and edited most of my videos. Frank Allen (of the Searchers) and Alan Lovell (of the Swinging Blue Jeans) both good friends. 1950s Chart topper (*Butterfly*, *Fabulous* etc.), Charlie Gracie (1936 – 2022) one of the nicest guys in Rock 'n' Roll who I backed as a drummer, with Ron Barrett and Andy Pascoe, in 2014. Charlie first toured the UK in 1957 (and recorded before Elvis Presley!) Sadly he died during the production of this book, however, his son Charlie Junior and his wife Joan remain my friends today.

The late Michael (Mick) Clayton CC, my best friend in Cornwall and especially while we both served as local Politicians.

Most especially, my lifelong best friend, Martin Kennedy Bell who has always been there for me, never more so than when the Audit Commission undertook an investigation into Kerrier District Council while I was a serving Councillor.

Michael & Emily Tarrant of Webfooted Designs Ltd who have run my websites for many years and their contributions to get this book draft on computer. Also Andrew Mckenzie, author and Mackenzie historian for his help and advice. I must include my editor and publisher (and fellow musician!) Toni Carver of St Ives Printing & Publishing Company without whose invaluable help and encouragement, this book would never have been completed or published!

Finally, friends, acquaintances, relatives many of whom are mentioned in this book. And everyone who over the last 10-20 years or so who I've got to know via the Internet and Social Media (both of which have made the world a much smaller place) partly as an explorer of Cornwall, Devon & Dorset but mainly as a musical historian, musician and collector of old, rare and unusual electric guitars.

Lastly but not least and most importantly of all, my parents Eric & Elizabeth Mackenzie because, without them, I would not be here.

Guy Mackenzie.

Dedication

To my grandchildren
Scarlet, Gabriel, Cassiel and Grace
because one day they might wish to know more.

Contents

Foreword v

Introduction 9

Chapter 1: 1946 and All That, 1946-1948 13

Chapter 2: Calgary House, Isle of Mull, 1948-1976 15

Chapter 3: Sunningdale School, 1955-1959 29

Chapter 4: And So Onto Stowe School, 1960-1963 35

Chapter 5: Applegarth and Freedom, 1963-1964 41

Chapter 6: Schools Out and the Road to London, 1964 45

Chapter 7: London at Last, 1965 49

Chapter 8: Southampton Calling, 1965-1966 51

Chapter 9: London Again, 1966-1971 55

Chapter 10: All Change! 1972 61

Chapter 11: Clynol, High Wycombe and Fat Man's Toy! 1972-1978 63

Chapter 12: Stateside Calling, 1979-1981 73

Chapter 13: Back in the UK – Starting Over! 1981-1986 81

Chapter 14: War in the West (Cornwall, That Is!), 1986-1987 89

Chapter 15: Just for the Record Herland Farm Barns, Godolphin, 1988 95

Chapter 16: The End of the Beginning, 1989 97

Chapter 17: The Big Bangs of 1990
aka "The Man with his Stone!" 1989 – 1990 101

Chapter 18: Mackenzie saves Sally, Amanda hits London,
Herland Barns completed (Phew!) – 1990 105

Chapter 19: Wonderful World of Cornish Property, 1991 – 2022 109

Chapter 20: Glimpses into the Life of a Local Politician! 1991 – 2003 113

Chapter 21: Back on the Road Again 2012 – 2016 123

Chapter 22: The Guitar Collection, 2005 – 2022 127

Chapter 23: Glenmuick, 1948 – 2022 131

Chapter 24: Epilogue 135

Introduction

BY TRADITION Guy Mackenzie's family is descended from the Mackenzies of Suddie, and thus directly descended from the Mackenzies' ancient chiefs who were Barons of Kintail. However, more recent detailed research seems to indicate that, in fact, the line of descent is from the Mackenzies of Braemar (Dalmore) and thence from the Barons of Kintail via an earlier line of descent, although conclusive proof of this has yet to materialise. However, it is with confidence that Guy can trace his ancestry back to the marriage of William Mackenzie and Margaret Moir which took place at Slains, Aberdeenshire on 13th January 1737. Their great grandson was his great grandfather, James Thompson Mackenzie who was created 1st Baronet of Glenmuick just a few months before his death on 12th August 1890.

The Mackenzies were involved in the unsuccessful Jacobite rising of 1719, so perhaps this conflict holds a clue as to the lack of verification of Guy's true ancestry. In the 20th Century his family could have owned Sandringham, the deeds of which they once held as security for a loan.

James Thompson Mackenzie was born on 27th December 1818. A letter dated 24th March 1881, to his son Allan, states that he left for India at the age of 13. In India he made a considerable fortune before finally returning to the United Kingdom in his early 30s. Following his return, he set up business in London and considerably increased his fortune. Apart from homes in London and the Home Counties, he also bought the Estates at Kintail in 1868 and about a year later, Glenmuick Estate, near Ballater, Aberdeenshire which adjoins the Royal Estate at Balmoral.

James' eldest son, Guy's grandfather Allan Russell, became the 2nd Baronet of Glenmuick, following his father's death.

Allan was born in 1850 and married Lucy Davidson a daughter of Duncan Davidson of Tulloch, in 1874. Duncan Davidson was a favourite of Queen Victoria and a "larger than life character". He married 5 times and outlived 4 of his wives. He fathered 18 legitimate children and at least 30 illegitimate children. Unsurprisingly, he was known locally as "The Stag"! Today Tulloch Castle is a hotel reputedly haunted by "the green lady" who is said to be one of his daughters and, therefore, Guy's great aunt! Legend has it that she walked in on her father while he was with one of his mistresses! She was so shocked that she fled and ran down the stairs to fall and break her neck!

Guy says he once stayed in one of the haunted rooms at Tulloch Castle. He was on his own and claims that, although he never saw the ghost of his great aunt, he never felt alone and enjoyed a very good night's sleep!

Guy's aunt, Lucy Mackenzie was Allan Russell Mackenzie's eldest child. She was born in 1875 and married Victor Hay, Earl of Errol. Their eldest son, Josslyn, was born in 1901 and became the 22nd Earl of Errol in 1928. He moved to Kenya with his first wife in 1928 and quickly became involved with the group of expatriates who became known as the "Happy Valley Set". The set became notorious for drug use, drinking, adultery and promiscuity! In 1939, Josslyn started an affair with Diana, Lady Broughton which ended with him being shot dead in his car in early 1941. Diana's husband Sir Jock Delves Broughton was tried for his murder but was, controversially, acquitted. Speculation over the murder case continues to this day. Several books have been written about the killing, and the Happy Valley Set. The best known of these is probably *White Mischief* (1982) by *Sunday Times* journalist James Fox who researched the case with the literary critic Cyril Connolly in the late 1960s. The book formed the basis of the 1988 film also called *White Mischief* starring Charles Dance as Josslyn Errol, Guy's first cousin.

Josslyn's brother, Gilbert was born in 1903 and succeeded to the title of 6th Baron Kilmarnock. He became a successful businessman in the City (of London). Guy recalls that Gilbert was very kind to him when, as a young man, he first went to work in London. Today the name Kilmarnock is probably more associated with Gilbert's son, Alistair and his second wife, Hilary (Hilly) who was the former wife of novelist, Kingsley Amis. Alistair and Hilly came to live as butler and housekeeper to Kingsley Amis following his divorce from novelist, Elizabeth Jane Howard. This arrangement resulted in much comment in the press at that time!

On an historical note, the 4th Earl of Kilmarnock joined the Jacobite rising of 1745 and was captured following the disaster of Culloden in 1746. He became one of the last people to be executed on Tower Hill, London. Interestingly, his eldest son, James (who later became Earl of Errol), fought on the Government side!

Guy lost his uncle Allan Keith in World War I at the Battle of the Somme in 1916. He had married Louvima, daughter of Francis Knollys, the 1st Viscount Knollys. Francis Knollys was appointed private secretary to the Prince of Wales in 1870, an office he held until Edward became King Edward VII in 1901. Francis Knollys' mother was Elizabeth St Aubyn of Clowance. Today, by coincidence, Guy lives in Cornwall just a few miles from Clowance giving him, by chance, a Cornish connection!

Allan Keith's son, Alexander George Anthony (Tony) who became the 4th Baronet of Glenmuick was born in 1913. Following the death of his father, he was raised by Guy's cousins Ethel and Madge Logan. They were the daughters of Colonel Lennox Logan and James Thompson Mackenzie's daughter, Mary. Guy succeeded to the title, as 5th Baronet of Glenmuick, following Tony's death in 1993.

Guy Mackenzie's succession to the Baronetcy of Glenmuick was not straightforward as he had been born two years before his parents were married. However, following a two year legal battle fought by his father, the Court of The Lord Lyon on 13th October 1970, found "In law" that, after his father, Guy was then the "nearest lawful heir-presumptive to the Baronetcy". Consequently Guy's Arms were matriculated on 21st October 1970.

Shortly before his death in 1890, James Thompson Mackenzie had disinherited his eldest son, Guy's grandfather Sir Allan Mackenzie 2nd Baronet, as the result of a bitter dispute. His father considered Allan's lifestyle and expenditure extravagant whereas Guy's grandfather resented, in particular, the amount of money his father had lent to the Prince of Wales (later King Edward VII), around £100,000; equivalent to about £10.2 million in today's money. However, as security for this loan, James Thompson Mackenzie held the title deeds of Sandringham, the Royal Estate in Norfolk.

When James Thompson Mackenzie was dying he was in the south of England. Senior members of the family attended him leaving only the younger members of the Mackenzie family and servants resident at Glenmuick. Among them were Guy's cousins Ethel and Madge Logan, the daughters of the Baronet's eldest daughter Mary. The girls were then only 12 and 10 years old, respectively. When their grandfather died and news reached the Royal household, equerries were sent by the Prince of Wales. They arrived at Glenmuick saying that they had come to collect some papers.

The children and the Glenmuick servants were in awe of these representatives of the Royal household and allowed them to search through James' desk and papers. This they did and subsequently left. When the adults returned, they were told of this visit and immediately went to check James Thompson Mackenzie's papers. They then found that the title deeds of Sandringham were missing.

The Trustees did not – perhaps could not due to the circumstances? – call in the debt and the money was never repaid. The story was well known in Guy's family. Both his parents had mentioned it while his cousins, Ethel and Madge (Margaret) Logan – who later provided him with a 'home from home' at Stowe and during the start of his working life – often talked about it. They believed that the debt was never pursued by the Mackenzie family as they didn't want to cause upset with The Royal Family.

James Thompson Mackenzie, 1st Baronet of Glenmuick died near Brighton, his body was returned to his home for the funeral and was interred in the family vault at Glenmuick. Following his death there was a long and costly legal battle between Sir Allan Mackenzie and his father's Trustees. This was unresolved until Guy's grandfather's death in 1906 when his uncle, Victor Audley Falconer Mackenzie succeeded to the Estate becoming the 3rd Baronet of Glenmuick.

For Guy Mackenzie, 5th Baronet of Glenmuick, his heritage is fascinating but the life of a Scottish aristocrat was not for him. More a "child of the Swinging 60s" his life in: retail, marketing, semi-pro car dealing, drumming and rock gigging to finally becoming an avid guitar collector (an instrument he doesn't play!), Internet blogger, local councillor and property developer in West Cornwall has left him with an assortment of fascinating memories. They not only provide the reader with both amusing and, sometimes, disturbing anecdotes but also provide valuable insights into the decades he has successfully navigated.

James Thompson Mackenzie

Chapter 1

1946 and All That, 1946 – 1948

ILLEGITIMATE! I was born illegitimate. It was a big thing, back in the day. Not so now, thank goodness! When I was born at Rubislaw Nursing Home, Aberdeen on 6th October 1946 such a condition was regarded as scandalous. Particularly as my family were Scottish aristocracy and, in 1993, I became the 5th Baronet of Glenmuick. Somehow, apart from the circumstance of my birth, I have managed to avoid scandal. It is in my family heritage and several times I have brushed by it and in London's "Swinging Sixties" well – anything could have happened. Scandals were close but passed me by.

Originally, as my first birth certificate stated, I was James William Guy Robertson-McIsaac! My father, Eric Dighton Mackenzie, had inherited the Glenmuick Estate just eight miles from Balmoral from his brother Victor, the 3rd Baronet, in 1944

It wasn't until after the marriage of my parents on 15th November 1948 that my birth name was correctly re-registered as James William Guy Mackenzie. By which time, Glenmuick Estate had been sold. My father faced a legal and financial challenge for "enticement" from my mother's ex-husband (hard to comprehend today!) and my parents had moved to Calgary Castle (which we always called Calgary House) on the Isle of Mull. My father had to sell the Glenmuick Estate partly for financial reasons, including death duties. And, maybe, also because the "neighbours" at Balmoral didn't wish to be so closely associated with another scandal... this one involving my birth!

My Great Grandfather, James Thompson Mackenzie, was born in 1818. He was still under the age of 14 when he left Scotland and went to sea as a midshipman. He ended up in India where he made a fortune. He briefly returned to Scotland in his early 20s, then went back to India before finally returning again in his early 30s having considerably increased his fortune. Following his return, he set up in business in London. He had homes in England and bought the Estate at Kintail circa 1868 as he believed he was descended from the Barons of Kintail. And, in about 1869 he also purchased Glenmuick near Ballater, Aberdeenshire, which adjoins the Royal Estate at Balmoral.

In 1890, just 5 months before his death, James Thompson Mackenzie was created 1st Baronet of Glenmuick. However, shortly before his death he disinherited his eldest son, Allan Russell Mackenzie (my Grandfather) who became the 2nd Baronet following James's death. There followed a lengthy and very costly legal dispute which resulted in my Grandfather managing to hold onto Glenmuick Estate. Following his death in 1906, the Estate passed to his second son, Victor, as his eldest son, Allan James Reginald "Jim" had died in South Africa in 1903.

Victor died unmarried in 1944 and so the title then passed to the son of his brother (Allan Keith "Sloper" who had died at the Somme in 1916), Alexander George Anthony (Tony) became the 4th Baronet and, following his death on 5th January 1993, I became the 5th Baronet of Glenmuick. But it was my father, not Tony, who inherited Glenmuick Estate on Victor's death in 1944.

I never lived in the "big house" (The House of Glenmuick), and my home, for the first two years of my life, was the cottage on the Estate that my mother rented from my father!

First Photo of Guy with his mother, Elizabeth (who was then Robertson-McIsaac)

Guy, visiting the Ballater Highland Games possibly in 1948 when he would have been just 2 years old. Pictured (left to right): his cousin Madge Logan; his aunt Lucy, Countess of Errol; his mother Elizabeth and Guy. The cutting, is probably from *The Press & Journal*, Scotland's oldest newspaper. It is interesting to note that Elizabeth & Guy are referred to by their original names although Guy's parents married nine days prior to the 1948 Games which took place on November 24th.

Chapter 2

Calgary House, Isle of Mull, 1948 – 1976

AFTER MY PARENTS took the decision to sell Glenmuick, they looked round Scotland for a new home and eventually came to the Isle of Mull and saw Calgary Castle – as it was called then and later. It had a wonderful outlook over the white sands of Calgary Bay to the sea, but the price was £15,000 and it needed renovation. Consequently, they left an offer of £8,000 and forgot about it. Several weeks went by and, out of the blue, they had a letter from the selling agents – their offer had been accepted! No doubt the sellers decided, in the post-war economic recession, cash was king! Ironically the situation was similar when sixty years later, in 2018, my wife Sally and I considered buying back the property. It had been empty for some time and required renovation – no change there then!

We moved to Mull in late 1948, staying at the Western Isles Hotel, Tobermory until Calgary was ready to move into. The house itself was mainly Victorian and built in the 19th Century Scottish baronial style of a castle with battlements, turrets and a dry moat and included about 50 acres of land. In those days, the tarmac road ended at our gate which was the start of the driveway, about 400 yards long which led to the house. From our front gate, the main road which led to Treshnish and onto Torloisk, was un-surfaced.

In the early days my parents rented Calgary Farm and the farmhouse was just outside our gate with its land mainly at a lower level between our house and the sea and every year the local ploughing matches were held there. The competitors were the local farmers and crofters, and it was a wonderful sight watching the horses all decked out and competing to plough a furrow. My other memory of Calgary farmhouse is the fire there, I must have been about 7 years old, but I can't remember how badly damaged the farmhouse was although I attended along with, it seemed, lots of other people and helped getting furniture and effects out and putting them in the garden outside. Luckily it wasn't typical Mull weather so it

Calgary House, Isle of Mull

wasn't raining but I felt very important running in, grabbing some small item and running out again! I felt even more important when, along with everyone else, I was given a cup of tea as a thank you for helping!

The blacksmith's shop was just to the right of the entrance to the farmhouse. I can remember the heat of the furnace and watching the horses being shod by the blacksmith.

A little further away, towards Tobermory, was Calgary post office which was set back from the road. Miss MacQuarrie the postmistress was great friends with the local postman. However, there was an occasion when the postman won, as I recall, the football pools 3 times! Not huge amounts of money but wins nevertheless! His coupons, which were postmarked on the Friday before the football matches, always arrived at the pools office the following week. The police investigated to discover that he had used the post office franking machine to predate his pools entry when Miss MacQuarrie wasn't looking ! Last thing I heard was he spent 3 years in Barlinnie jail! Poor Miss MacQuarrie was absolutely distraught and, looking back, I wonder if she ever got over it as not long afterwards the post office was closed.

I remember visiting one of the local jails, in Salen between Craignure and Tobermory with my father. The policeman showed us round. It was empty except for his potatoes which he kept there as it was cool. I still wonder what he did with them if he ever had to use it for the purpose it had been built!

In those early days, I had a Nannie (called Nannie Sangster) who I remember came from Stonehaven, south of Aberdeen on the Scottish mainland. Although I know I loved her very much, all I can remember of her was that she was quite short, cuddly and very kind. After Lucy, my sister, was born in 1949, evidently I said to Nannie Sangster: "Let's run away together so we're away from Lucy!" Of course we didn't but it must have seemed a great idea at the time! Perhaps to reinforce that wish, my earliest memory of Lucy is pushing her over, which cut her leg and made her cry! My father was not amused and I remember him taking me into his study (which we called the Smoking Room – he had smoked but gave up when he married my mother) putting me over his knee and spanking me which resulted in me hiding in a cupboard!

I often wonder if Lucy ever got over it? I think so, as now she has created, from

An early picture of Nannie Sangster holding Guy

nothing over a period of 20 or so years, a fabulous garden and nursery, about 8 miles from Calgary, which is now the 2nd most popular tourist attraction on Mull after Duart Castle! Lucy has also been featured in several publications and on TV! Her daughter, my niece, Vittoria, is a World Class Event Rider.

We visited other islands such as historic, Inch Kenneth, then owned by Lady Redesdale (mother of the Mitford Sisters). Also, the huge Island of Ulva which was tragically romanticised by Thomas Campbell in his poem *Lord Ullin's Daughter* when he visited Mull in 1792. I don't think we ever managed to walk its length although Lucy tells me she has done this recently. And, several times, we visited the Island of Staffa with its remarkable basalt columns. Of course, whilst there, we always went into Fingal's Cave made famous firstly by Sir Joseph Banks (who named it), and others including Queen Victoria, plus Felix Mendelssohn who wrote his overture after visiting it. But, unsurprisingly, we stayed away from Eorsa which was supposedly inhabited by "serpents" who put paid to the last inhabitants!

Back in 1948, at Calgary House, there was a large walled garden at a lower level to the house and attached to the back wall was a cottage. Archie, our gardener,

Guy's Mother, Elizabeth Katherine Mary (1918 – 2002) pictured as a young mum with Lucy, in the early days at Calgary (circa late 1949/early 1950). Later she became a respected and knowledgeable gardener who created the magical woodland garden at Calgary. She also wrote articles for gardening magazines and was widely recognised for her horticultural achievements resulting in her first being invited, in 1970, to the Women of Scotland Luncheon.

lived here with his brother, John. Archie came with the house. He was there when we arrived and stayed with us until both he and his brother had died. His cottage had no mains electricity and Calgary house didn't either, just a generator. Mains water was completely absent. Ours came from the same burn as Archie's but from a higher level. I believe that they'd lived there all their lives and I remember Archie always being friendly and cheerful.

In the house we had Ella, who my mother always said she'd first met wandering through (living in?) the wood that formed part of our land, who became our housekeeper. My mother had a natural talent for cooking and had been trained at the Cordon Bleu School in London and so was an excellent cook. Under my mother's tuition Ella became our cook and she stayed with us until my mother sold up in 1976.

I was always great friends with Ella but never more than when I became a Scottish Football fanatic, and a Rangers supporter, as her nephew played for Kilmarnock, a leading Scottish club. Of course, Ella (being a Macdonald), had no time for the Campbell clan as, even then, some 200 years later, the Massacre of Glencoe hadn't been forgotten or forgiven!

Guy's parents in the 1950s

In the early days we also had one or two local girls to help in the house, although I recall them both becoming pregnant in quick succession and leaving when their children were born to bring up their families. Later on my mother employed students to help in the summer holidays.

In 1952, my brother Allan was born. I remember him being quiet and studious but don't especially remember pushing him over, although I'm sure that I did!

In later life Allan has become very successful in the world of Real Estate in the USA, after gaining an Honours Degree from Cambridge University. In 1985 I was both delighted and honoured to be asked to be his best man (despite many of his close friends being there) at his fabulous 1985 San Diego wedding to Robin. I was also able to visit his first property development. A $50m office block!

Was I a good elder brother to Allan and my sister Lucy? Well apart from claiming the 5th Amendment (the right to remain silent) I'll just say, sometimes in life two's company but three's a crowd and it sometimes was! Want to know more? You'll have to ask them! But they've both made huge successes of their lives and I'm very proud of them!

I always admired my father. I remember him as being both kind and honourable and very well organised as one would expect from someone who was not only Colonel of his Regiment, in the Scots Guards, but also Comptroller of the Household of the Governor General of Canada between the first and second world wars, he fought in both!

He was nearly twice my mother's age at 54, she was 28, when I was born and slightly Victorian in outlook. He always had a list of things to do on his desk (and I'm using his desk now!) and ticked them off as they were completed! After a few years he bought Antium Farm near Dervaig (having given up the tenancy of Calgary Farm), which had a few fields but was effectively a hill farm of 3,000 acres suitable only for sheep – and then only suitable for about one per acre. In this day and age, this sounds a huge acreage but, in reality it was less than one tenth of the size of the largest estate on Mull which was, in fact, a holiday home for its owner – a Member of the House of Lords!

Every day, my father would go to the farm to collect fresh milk, butter and eggs and quite often I went with him. I really enjoyed this as he seemed to relax when it was just the two of us, making silly remarks followed up by: "Don't tell your mother," which kept me amused throughout the journey. Then, once a week, he drove to Tobermory (just 12 miles but a 40 minutes drive then!) for the household shopping.

I always enjoyed these journeys as well. Especially once I began getting pocket money which started at sixpence per week, about 2.5p in today's money; although you could get a lot more for your money back then. Nails! I spent all my pocket money on nails. From these childhood shopping trips you can date my lifelong interest in building! Already my first building project, a

Guy's parents in the late 1960s

"house" built behind the wooden seat near our front lawn had begun. Exhibiting extraordinary originality, I called it "my house"! Later on I built two tree houses and another house. My interest in property development not only started at a very early age – but it was definitely "hands on"!

In the early days, my father always drove a van but he did, for a short time, own a black car. I remember it being very dusty and with a stick I drew a picture on the boot! I was actually very pleased with my drawing and asked him to come and look at it. As you can imagine, he was not impressed, in fact, rather the opposite!

My father was a whisky drinker who very often had a whisky and soda at his right hand. His preference was for either Black & White or an Islay single malt. In my father's time, Mull had no whisky distilleries unlike the Isle of Islay, just half the size of Mull, but now boasting 9 distilleries! You can't be born a Scot and not love a whisky so I'll have a 10 year old highland malt, please! He was always generous and known for his highland hospitality which he extended to anyone who visited the house and did any work for us. Afterwards, he would disappear with that person into his study and they'd have a wee dram or two together. This was demonstrated when, several years later, I found myself in the beer tent at the Salen Agricultural Show. The person next to me at the bar asked me where I was from and when I said Calgary he asked me if I knew Col. Mackenzie. Of course, I was using my best highland accent at the time and replied, aye, I do. My fellow drinker then said: "I like the Colonel, but I like his drams better!" I left shortly after, just in case my cover was blown!

The local primary school was about 2 miles away but had only 2 pupils. One was the son of the school teacher, who was the same age as me and I knew slightly, and the other was a girl, who I also knew, who was about 3 years younger! But my parents chose to send me, at about the age of 6, to Mrs. Mackenzie, who was a retired school teacher who lived about half a mile away.

I really don't remember much about her teaching but I do remember always walking to and from her house. In those days there was almost no traffic and so the walk was always safe, with the exception of the wild animals I had to often walk past on the track which adjoined our land en route to the road. They were terrifying animals, and huge too, and I daren't walk past them if they were on the track. Consequently I used to go back to our garden to find our gardener (we

Guy building his first tree house circa.1958

always had one) to frighten the animals away! While I might like to claim that these terrifying creatures, the sum of all my fears, were either deer, wild goats or something more exotic I have to admit that they were sheep! Well, they were huge and frightening to this six year old anyway!

I remember my mother as being hugely energetic and a very hard worker. She would charge around Calgary House with its two staircases, up one and down the other, singing as she went. Her favourite song was The Star of the County Down and it's one of my favourites now. Over the years it has been covered by hundreds of singers including a great version by Van Morrison which he recorded on his 1988 album Irish Heartbeat and it can be easily found on YouTube. I often play along to it on my drums, thinking of her as I do. I often wish that the people who knew my mother in her last few years when she was so disabled with arthritis could have seen her then!

In contrast to my father who was always early for any appointment (or train) my mother, a bit like me, was always running late – especially for lunch which was always served at 1pm. I remember his obvious frustration when at five or even ten past one, there was no sign of her! Then she would arrive, full of apologies but my father was always the perfect gentleman, hid his annoyance and never really complained!

With Calgary sands so near, we were encouraged to learn to swim at an early age and also spent a lot of time on the beach in summer, even if it wasn't very warm! When I was about 9 years old my parents bought us a small boat which we called Tamarisk, I think it was 10 footer. I was sent off to Mrs. Mackenzie's husband to be taught about boats and boating. We knew him as the Commander, as he was an ex-naval Commander and was well known locally for his expertise. When he felt that I'd learned enough, I was allowed out with Lucy and Allan to row in Calgary Bay and fish for mackerel. We also had a few lobster pots and actually did catch some. Looking back, although we had life jackets, we seldom wore them! It's amazing to think that we survived, because there's a lot of ocean and little else between Calgary and the USA so, when a storm suddenly blew up, as it did sometimes, it was often quite hazardous returning to shore avoiding the reefs!

Later on we had a 14' boat with a Seagull outboard motor which we called *Tyche*. Some of our trips in this were even more hazardous as we went round Treshnish Point to the Island of Gometra! We also went as far as the Treshnish Islands which were then owned by my parents' friends, Niall

Lucy and Allan aboard *Tyche* in Calgary Bay

Rankin, explorer, ornithologist and writer and his wife, Lady Jean Rankin who was Lady in Waiting to the Queen Mother! Looking back, Lucy and Allan always seemed to trust me as I was the Captain, having been promoted by the Commander! He always said that the crew must do whatever the Captain commands them to do, even if told to jump overboard! Fortunately I never found it necessary to do this

On an historical note, Lady Jean had played a "pivotal role" during Princess Margaret's fraught relationship with Group Captain Peter Townsend, acting as go-between, counsellor especially during the sad period after the Princess decided to call off their engagement. Interestingly, and having looked through the Glenmuick guest books, both their signatures appear in October 1945 and 1946 along with the then Queen and her daughter, our late Queen Elizabeth II.

My mother was very adventurous and loved exploring new places (as I do today) and, in the early days we might go as far as the Treshnish Cave or possibly the Whisky Cave at Burgh which had the remains of an illicit whisky still. We also loved visiting Mackinnon's Cave.

The story here was that the cave went through the island and a piper had once gone in with his dog, while playing his pipes. After a while there was a wail of pipes and the piper was never seen again but his dog reappeared out of a hole in the ground 10 miles away! This was a real adventure as the cave could only be visited at low tide. However, and like Dr Johnson & Boswell about 200 years earlier we never got further than MacLeod's Table which was a huge table shaped rock about 400 yards in, as there had been a massive rock fall which blocked the cave from then on. Never-the-less we used to fantasise that one day we'd get some help and clear the fall and find out how far back the cave went. Of course we never did and probably lots of others have wanted to do the same, but, as far as I am aware, they haven't either – so the mystery of the piper remains.

Macleod's Table in Mackinnon's cave with L to R: Guy, Sarah Stuart & Allan

The Chapel of the Fishing Nets

Allan at the Marble Quarry on Iona

My mother took us to lots of other exciting places including the very long walk to Carsaig Arches and the Chapel of the Fishing Nets. This was a remote net loft with a chapel set out inside on the upstairs floor which was supposedly haunted! Sadly we never saw this ghost nor that of "Headless Ewen" who was said to be seen riding his horse with his head under his arm near Lochbuie House and Moy Castle when a Maclaine of Lochbuie died! And, of course, she took us to Iona where we walked along Bloody Bay, once the scene of a battle; the spouting cave watching as it threw up plumes of spray through a hole in its roof and also visited the Marble Quarry.

Occasionally there were children's parties on Mull, very often they were held at the Anderson's house near Tobermory. The Andersons had 4 children who were similar ages to us but, as their parents were really first class Scottish dancers, they were too! Unlike any of us as, apart from anything else, neither of my parents were enthusiastic dancers, actually, my father not at all! So I usually felt a bit out of things at these parties as I always ended up being pushed through an Eightsome Reel, *The Duke of Perth* or *Strip The Willow* by Mrs. Anderson. I can still hear her saying: "Now set to your partner, Guy, swing her round, now a figure of eight... then a teapot... etc, etc." All still a bit of a mystery to me although I did attend the Oban Ball twice in later years but I must have had some training beforehand as there were some brilliant dancers there and somehow I managed to fit in!

I was also invited by the Queen to a dinner and dance at Holyrood House, Edinburgh where I had one dance with Princess Anne! But I always regretted not asking the Queen to dance who seemed to be standing, talking rather more than dancing but, like several other young men there, we weren't brave enough to do so!

Some years ago, my wife Sally and I joined a Scottish Dancing Society in Cornwall and, although the standard wasn't as high as at a Highland Ball, we decided that it was still beyond our abilities! But I loved watching the musicians playing Scottish dance music and the drummer playing in a military style with perfect drum rolls – which is something I still can't do properly today!

My mother was a very keen and dedicated gardener and over the years, having transformed our formal walled garden (which also provided most of our fruit and vegetables), started to turn part of our wood into a Woodland Garden. She worked incredibly hard over many years, in all weathers, and with the help of her dedicated gardener, it became the acclaimed Woodland Garden (occasionally open to the Public) that many people still remember today. Very sadly, none of the subsequent owners have kept things going but, despite that, it's still exciting to wander through my mother's Woodland Garden and still see some of the exotic trees, plants and shrubs she planted all those years ago. After she died, Lucy placed a small memorial stone dedicated to our mother in a quiet peaceful place near the burn which runs through the Woodland Garden and we scattered some of her ashes nearby.

My Father was kind and generous and through him I met another true gentleman, Alf Ramsey — later Sir Alf Ramsey — manager firstly of Ipswich Town FC and then of the England team which won the World Cup in 1966.

My father always hated football but, knowing my love for the game (and especially Scottish football) bought tickets for us to attend a Scotland vs. England game at Hampden Park, Glasgow. It was a fabulous day and one I'll never forget especially as I recall Scotland winning 3-1 so it must have been 1964. After an early dinner in Glasgow, I took the sleeper train back to London and who should be in my carriage, none other than Alf Ramsey and a couple of England players (how times change!). Of course I had to ask him for his autograph which I still have. But I'll always remember his polite manner and the time he took to speak to this "cock a hoop" young Scotsman. What a delightful gentleman!

When I was about 15 one of the local crofters, offered to give me his motorcycle, a 1939 BSA 350cc, as he never used it because it was missing the magneto. He'd been unable to get a replacement so was about to throw it over a cliff! (In fact that's what happened to quite a lot of unwanted things on Mull – including cars when they'd passed their sell-by date! In Cornwall it was mine shafts!). I knew nothing about motorcycles at that time but it was the start of a passion that has stayed with me all my life - although I haven't ridden one for some time, despite owning a Kawasaki Drifter 900cc (a modern copy of an Indian Chief – one of the most sought after bikes of its day) now! Of course I never managed to get hold of the missing part but when I was 16 my parents bought me a BSA 250cc C11 for £18 which I absolutely loved. Of course being British and quite old, it was always

Guy trying to 'do the ton' around Calgary House

breaking down but, when it was running, it was great fun and I remember giving a quite brave girl who was on holiday a ride on the pillion down an unmade road. I went as fast as possible, which was only about 30 mph, but seemed like 100 to her! Back then we didn't wear helmets and when we stopped she was visibly shaking and just like someone later mentioned in my "Assorted Memories", she was determined never to get on the back of any motorcycle again, let alone one with me driving!

When I'd left school, I had several of my friends to stay including Martin Bellamy who gamely came boating with us, despite never having been aboard a small boat – there isn't much sea in Gloucestershire! I also remember inviting a girlfriend who my mother took an instant dislike to and called her, but not to her face, Miss Piggy! Up till then I hadn't noticed a likeness as the girl had other attributes! But once my mother pointed it out to me and reinforced her opinion by mimicking her walk (mainly when the girl wasn't watching!) I started to see the connection and once noticed, within a matter of days following our return South, Miss P. was, as they say, consigned to "history"!

I always spent Christmas at Calgary until I got married and I'll always remember Christmas there as a magical time. It started on Christmas Eve while listening to the Service of 9 Lessons and Carols, which I still do, while we put up and decorated the tree and we always added some real candles in antique holders along with the decorations. And, of course, we lit them too – goodness only knows how we didn't set the tree (or the house itself) alight but somehow we didn't! Later

Guy in his Sumbeam Alpine IV at Calgary in 1971 before his life changed

on when we got mains electricity we had tree lights as well, but never stopped using the candles.

When we woke up on The Day we opened our stockings and, after breakfast, went to Gruline Church for the Christmas Service. My parents weren't overly religious but did attend at Easter as well. We were always careful where we sat in Church as some families had their own designated pews and once we had sat in the one reserved for the Macleans of Duart, the leading family on the Island!

The Islands of Mull, Coll, Tiree and Jura are some of inherited lands of Clan Maclean and the seat of the Clan Chief is Duart Castle. At the time this was Sir Charles Maclean Bt., later created Lord Maclean. Sometime later that year, Lady Maclean mentioned to my mother that someone had been sitting in their pew, much to my mother's embarrassment! But, knowing Lady Maclean a little better now – a remarkable lady who drove herself to London the day after I saw her last, aged nearly 90. I am sure her comment, all those years ago, was just teasing rather than a serious criticism!

After the service it was back for lunch which was fresh (!) roast turkey with all the trimmings and afterwards opening the presents which were always placed under the tree. It was always such a happy time and one which I've never forgotten.

Guy (left) wearing a Glenmuick tweed jacket pictured with Lucy, Allan and their mother's car at Calgary in 1969

Calgary House was full of character and was a welcoming and happy family home. It may have been cold, damp, draughty and with only a crackly radio reception until TV arrived in 1968, but I could never wait to return for the holidays.

And I'll always remember watching the sun setting on the sea beyond Calgary Bay. I absolutely loved living at Calgary and I'm just so grateful to my parents for an idyllic upbringing which I've never forgotten, on the magical Island of Mull and even today, I still think of Calgary House as my home.

Guy's Father, Colonel Eric Dighton Mackenzie, (1891 – 1972)
A perfect gentleman

Island life: Guy carrying a sheep on Mull, the idyllic home of his childhood

Mackinnon's Cave, a favourite exploration site for Guy and his siblings

Chapter 3
Sunningdale School, 1955 – 1959

IN JANUARY 1955 I went off to school. In my case it was to Sunningdale prep school in Berkshire, England, which was a 36-hour journey away from Mull. Now, as everyone who knows me knows, I hate getting up early and this trip necessitated me getting up at 7.15 (early for me!) to catch the boat (the *M.V. Lochinvar*) to Oban and then the sleeper train to London. And, on the following day, the train from London to Sunningdale, eventually arriving at school in the late afternoon just in time for tea!

In those days, the *Lochinvar* made one return trip every day from Mull to Oban and it had a capacity of just 4 cars per trip – provided each car safely negotiated the 2 wire netting baskets and then was craned onto the boat or alternatively, as occasionally happened, the car would end up in the sea!

The *Lochinvar* brought back a lot of memories for me as it was the only way on or off Mull when I first lived there. It was also named after my favourite poem *Lochinvar* by Sir Walter Scott and even had paintings by J. Carey of each verse framed and hung on the walls of the saloon. I loved looking at them whenever I was on board. Recently I was successful in tracking down the beautiful paintings of the poem *Lochinvar* which I heard had been saved after the ship was sold. I now have photographs of them all.

On one trip and as a young boy, my father and I were invited by the Captain to come up to the bridge. He actually allowed me to steer the ship for a short time before grabbing the wheel to stop me steering it off course! I also remember asking him if it would ever sink! His reply was: "No, the *Lochinvar* will never sink". However, sadly and many years later after it had been sold and renamed *Anzio*, it did sink and with the loss of all the 13 crew off the coast of Lincolnshire!

We caught the boat at Salen, then to Lochaline (on the mainland) then the *Lochinvar*'s next stop was Craignure where it was met by a small motorboat before continuing on to Oban where we finally arrived several hours after embarking at Salen. Of course, we always admired Duart Castle (home of the Chiefs of the Clan Macleans) after leaving Craignure and then marvelled at the Lady Rock (which was submerged at high tide) where one of the chiefs had left his wife at low tide hoping never to see her again. However, she survived much to his surprise when she appeared at his celebratory dinner that same evening!

After reaching Oban it was a long wait for the sleeper train and this often necessitated a change of trains at Crianlarach to catch the through train from Fort William to Kings Cross or Euston which arrived about 7.30am. My parents accompanied me on this first trip, thereafter I was put on the train at Oban or Crianlarach (my father would tip the sleeper car attendant to look after me), and

I was met in London then taken and put on the train to School. Amazing to think, in this day and age, I usually travelled 2nd class which meant sharing the sleeping car with a second male traveller (who I'd of course, never met) or even 3rd class which meant sharing the sleeping car with 3 others and sometimes mixed sexes too! Thankfully, in those far-off days nothing untoward ever happened. Would it be the same today – I wonder? Not that this would be acceptable now!

When I first arrived at Sunningdale, it seemed that I'd never seen so many boys in one place! The school was a large Victorian building set in large grounds with its own chapel and swimming pool as well as playing fields.

It had about 80 pupils which was probably about as many as there were on the whole of Mull! It was a culture shock for a child from a remote island and I hated saying goodbye to my parents. I also missed my home and the sound of the sea.

I must admit for the first few nights I cried myself to sleep. Fortunately, I soon realised that the other boys of my age were friendly and understanding and the school itself had a welcoming atmosphere. Very soon I made friends who would remain as friends throughout my time there.

The headmaster was Mr Sheepshanks, who we referred to as 'Sheepy'. Everyone had a nickname and mine was 'Mull'. As I recall, Sheepy always wore a green checked suit and brown suede shoes. He was short, slightly effeminate and spoke with a lisp. My mother always contended that Sheepy didn't like my father, who was tall and distinguished and, with his military bearing, very much the opposite of my headmaster. However, the school was well run and although Sheepy was quite strict we always felt that he was fair despite having a strong right arm when wielding the cane! He also had a very attractive wife who was always pleasant to us boys and she had a friendly smile.

Next in line was Mr Burrows ('Budgie') who I always got on well with. Budgie was in charge of football which I grew to love, partly thanks to his encouragement and coaching, eventually being awarded my 'colours' in 1958. This was very exciting and always a complete surprise. After a match with another school, the captain of football would come into the school dining room during supper and place a cap on the head of the boy receiving this honour saying, in my case: "Well played Mackenzie," and the whole school would applaud! Something I'll never forget.

Then there was Mr Squarey (no nickname needed) who was in charge of cricket and a real enthusiast too! He always seemed to carry an umbrella. Whenever one walked past him we would say "Good morning" or "Good afternoon, Sir" his reply would be something like: "Always keep a straight bat" or "Through the covers" followed by the appropriate cricket shot played with his umbrella! I must have paid attention to this coaching as I ended up as Captain of the 2nd Eleven! OK, not the highest accolade, I know!

There was also Mr. Dawson who, in due course, bought the school in partnership with his brother. His son, Tom, now owns and runs the school. I remember Mr. Dawson ('Dawsey') having a brand new MG TF which was black with a soft top which we boys much admired – as did Dawsey! One day a hole appeared in the soft top, obviously burned with the aid of the sun through a magnifying glass! Understandably Dawsey was furious and although no one owned up to doing it – I always had the distinct impression that he blamed me! I shall now confirm, once and for all, over 60 years later, that it really wasn't me – honest! The appalling incident remains an unsolved mystery.

The one female teacher, Miss Paterson ('Patey'), I recall as being rather stern and, no, I never did well with French – several years later failing my French O Level 5 times! Is that a record, I wonder?

The only member of staff I didn't like was the Matron, Pauline, who seemed to be one of the most unsympathetic people I've ever met! I recall the excruciating pain of having a splinter of wood down a finger nail and when I asked her to get it out, her reply was – it's too far in you'll just have to let it work itself out. Arrrr!

Guy's Cadillac – pictured in 1989

I made good friends at Sunningdale. My best friends were: Charles Fairey who was the grandson of the aviation pioneer, Richard Fairey. The Fairey Swordfish, Fairey Gannet and, of course, the Fairey Delta II which famously achieved a world speed record of 1,132 mph in 1956! This was a really exciting connection, not just for us boys, but the whole school!

Jeremy Sykes was the second son of Sir Richard Sykes, of Sledmere Hall, Yorkshire. I went to stay there a couple of times and always admired the fact that Jeremy's father had 6 cars and one was a '59 Cadillac convertible with huge fins! For years afterwards I lusted after one and finally managed to buy a slightly later model for $500 in the States in 1980 which I imported into the UK and kept for over 10 years and, although it only did 10 mpg, I still regret selling it!

Reggie Sheffield ('Sleepy') is better known today as the father of Samantha Cameron, wife of our former Prime Minister, David Cameron!

The other boys included: Prince Michael of Kent who was much older than me and who seemed quite grand and aloof. Carey Harrison, younger son of the famous actor, Rex Harrison (star of *My Fair Lady, Doctor Dolitte* etc., etc.). I thought his then wife, actress and star of the film *Genevieve*, Kay Kendall was the most beautiful woman I'd ever seen. Tragically she died of leukaemia aged just 33 and I remember being very upset when I heard the sad news of her death.

I found Douglas Hogg (now Viscount Hailsham) rather studious and reserved as a schoolboy. Years later he became infamous for 'charging the public purse' £2,000 for cleaning the moat on his estate in the Parliamentary Expenses scandal of 2010! Silly man – I've been longing to say that!

One of the things to look forward to was being 'taken out' by parents or relatives for the day on occasional weekends. I especially remember going out with Charles Fairey's father who was married to a very beautiful lady called Atalanta and lived in a fabulous Thames-side home. We always went for lunch at the Hinds Head in Bray and, for the first time in my life, I ate smoked salmon sandwiches. This was a real treat in those post war days and one which I still really enjoy. A drink of non-alcoholic Pimms would complete the treat! Then we would go back to his home and occasionally Charles and I (when we were older) would be allowed to take out his father's very smart Thames launch (with a sloping rear) on the river on our own! I do recall powering through a speed limited section of the Thames and being shouted at by others as we sped past them! Great fun!

I also remember with affection my uncle 'Twitch' Thomas Innes, my mother's younger brother taking me out and loading me up with packets of sweets which I smuggled back into school. This was against the rules as we were only allowed 2

Guy's Uncle 'Twitch'

a day and 3 on a Saturday! Sadly uncle Twitch died in a car accident when still only in his 30s.

My mother especially loved cats and we always had cats at Calgary. In fact, at one time we had 5! I remember especially Toby, Lucy's beautiful black and white cat which, as I recall, lived to a ripe old age. However I can still remember how devastated I'd been at Sunningdale, aged about 10, on hearing from my mother of the sudden death of my much loved Timmy Willy who was only aged 2! But I also remember the kindness of my friends there at that sad time.

Regarding school work itself (the main reason I was there) I really can remember very little! I did quite well in Latin (really useful in this day and age!) but not much else. This was demonstrated by the fact that I got 'middle fourth' in my Common Entrance exams for Eton – which was effectively (and actually!) a failure grade. Most of the boys at Sunningdale went on to Eton and certainly I had hoped to do so but, having failed, my parents had to find an alternative school that would accept me. And that school turned out, unfortunately, to be Stowe which, at that time, had a 'bad reputation' which even my friends knew about! They were concerned for me and, although we promised to keep in contact. I never saw any of them ever again… Sunningdale was a wonderful happy school but it didn't prepare me for what was to come, nor should it have done.

Chapter 4

And so onto Stowe School, 1960 – 1963

STOWE IS SITUATED in the Buckinghamshire countryside and is, without doubt, one of the finest country houses in England. It is set in several hundred acres of landscaped gardens with follies, grottos, temples, towers and artificial lakes and became a school in the 1920s as a way of saving the property for posterity. There is much about Stowe on the Internet and today all indications are that it is a first class school which, now, also accepts girls. But in my day, there weren't any girls, just about 600 boys aged between about 13 and 18. And, of course, this was before Richard Branson's time there as I'd left before he arrived.

It was strange, looking back, that my friends at Sunningdale (then aged about 12!) knew about Stowe's 'bad reputation' for what would now come under the all-encompassing heading of 'abuse' and, later, when I worked briefly in a factory in Buckingham my work mates there were a bit more forthright saying things like: "Stowe's full of queers (homosexuals – illegal at that time!) from the headmaster down!". Of course that wasn't entirely correct but, while I was there, lurid rumours about teaching staff did circulate followed, in one case, by a quick and unexplained departure, so maybe the opinion in Buckingham wasn't entirely wrong!

As most people now know and partly as a result of the Independent Enquiry into Child Sexual Abuse and other similar investigations, there were many boarding schools and institutions, at that time in the UK, with similar issues and some were much worse!

My parents knew something of the school's reputation but my mother explained to me that the previous headmaster had had a climbing accident in Skye, some 5 years previously and soon after he had been appointed. He had never fully recovered from the head injuries he sustained. As a consequence, the school had gone 'downhill'. However, she also told me, that the Governors had just appointed a very bright new Headmaster, Donald Crighton Miller (DCM), who would turn things round! No doubt, word of Stowe's reputation had eventually reached the ears of the Governing body and they had decided enough was enough! Unfortunately, and over time, it became obvious to us that this was not to be the case as DCM never had the support of the senior staff and, as a result, he was effectively sacked just after my departure from the school.

Quite simply parts of the school were out of control, some houses were run by the boys, many senior Masters (teachers) were ineffectual and didn't want to change or be changed!

By one of those strange coincidences that sometimes happen, many years later when I found myself in conflict with a riding school, which had been franchised by a Cornish holiday park owned by Rank Plc., over the death of my wife's horse,

I ended up negotiating compensation with Angus Crighton Miller who was the responsible Board Director of Rank and owners of the park who was, in fact, DCM's son! I was able to discuss with him his father's experiences at Stowe which were exactly as I have outlined above.

But I've digressed and so back to the beginning…

Somehow when I first arrived, Stowe didn't seem to have the same welcoming atmosphere as Sunningdale, nobody I met seemed especially friendly and there appeared to be an air of foreboding about the place. If I'd thought the 80 or so boys at Sunningdale a culture shock, to be in the middle of 600 was quite simply, overwhelming!

Nevertheless, I found my way to my new house, Nugent, where I spent my first term waiting for a vacancy in my allocated house, Cobham. In fact and apart from being threatened by another 'new boy' with a razor knife (something I've never seen or heard of before then) on my first day, my first term went reasonably well.

In my second term I moved into Cobham house. The housemaster was Mr Brown ('DIB') whose claim to fame appeared to be that he had played rugby for Scotland. However, that time seemed to be well behind him as he had developed an enormous stomach which appeared to be supported by the braces which held up his trousers and it was this which one first became aware of when he entered a room! His deputy was Mr Vinen who seemed to me like one of the actor Ian Carmichael's characters from an Ealing comedy such as *I'm All Right Jack*. The type of person who was totally ineffectual.

Neither of them lived in Cobham house so during or before 'prep' in the evening when whichever of them was on duty had left, the boys were left in control until the following morning! This was when the bullying started and, of course, it was the new boys who came in for the worst punishment as they were the smallest! Unfortunately for me, I seemed to be the main target although Martin Bellamy (who became a friend) and one other (who cleverly learned to deflect attention from himself by becoming a comic) acted as reserves! No one in authority (especially DIB who was far too lazy and disinterested) wanted to intervene as it was simply considered a rite of passage, maybe a way of passing the time and, after all, everyone had gone through it to some extent anyway!

Tom Brown's Schooldays but without the open fire – luckily!

I'm still not sure why I was their main target but maybe because I'd been prepared for Eton (most Sunningdale boys went on to Eton) which was a school many despised! This had become clear in my first term when Stowe had played Eton in a friendly rugby match. The shouts from the Stowe touchline and the levels of violence meted out to the Etonians, who didn't play rugby, was obviously alarming to them and to me too as I've never forgotten that day! Quite simply Stowe seemed to have a massive "chip on its shoulder" and many of the boys, quite simply, felt inferior to the Etonians.

During my second and to a lesser extent in my third and fourth terms, Stowe became a fight for survival. In due course, I started to realise that the best way to combat bullying was to fight back, whatever the odds, which I started to do and on one occasion a lucky kick from me knocked out two front teeth of one of my attackers (one down 10 to go!) – he never troubled me again! In due course Martin Bellamy and another helped to, somewhat, even up the score too… which spoilt the fun!

Of course, as time went on, there was a new intake of boys to pick on. But the 'culture' in Cobham did seem to start to change the following year and there was a new tougher housemaster on the way as well.

The main reason for me being at Stowe was, of course, to learn and be given a first class start in life! Amazing as it seems now, I simply can't remember the names of any masters who taught me nor can I remember going to any classrooms at all. Was the teaching any good? In retrospect they must have been an uninspiring bunch especially as I can still clearly remember several of the teaching staff at Sunningdale! And, it was probably more due to Budgie (Mr Burrows) than any teaching at Stowe, that I did get Latin O Level!

Of course my school reports were appalling, with the words 'weak' and 'poor' appearing regularly regarding my grasp of the various subjects on offer. 'Taught' is the wrong word! I know my parents were concerned about me and my father threatened to send me to Oban High School if my reports didn't improve. I knew he'd had a tough schooling and always remember him telling me that he'd once found 7 slugs in his salad at prep school. He had to eat them all as they were on his plate! Sometimes I've wondered how different my life might have been if I'd been educated at Eton or, for that matter, Oban High School!

I knew that my mother and my cousins, Ethel and Madge Logan who lived near Buckingham and took me out occasionally at weekends, were worried too. My mother asked me about Stowe several times but I just couldn't talk about it and simply blotted it out of my mind for many years. Since my mother died, I have found some correspondence between her and Donald Crighton Miller – although I can't help feeling from his letters that he probably didn't know who I was and, in any case, he had pressing issues of his own to deal with!

It wasn't until I went to the States that I first started to face up to my first year or so at Stowe. In reality, I wasn't able to put it behind me until many years later when I became an elected local politician in Cornwall in 1993 and also a residential landlord with a 'Supporting People' Accreditation (a scheme introduced by Tony Blair's government) both of which gave me the opportunity to help others perhaps less fortunate than me.

But as time went on Stowe did result in some positives for me… The first was music. Someone who I became friendly with later on was David Moores (now the Ex-Chairman of Liverpool FC) who'd seen the Beatles in Liverpool and brought them to Stowe in April 1963 for a fee of £100! Martin Bellamy and I both saw them as did the whole school and, afterwards, I got their autographs which I still have today. I was transfixed and this resulted in music being my main hobby since and a part time job for many years too.

The second is my love of follies and unusual buildings and Stowe had plenty of those! At that time many were unsafe, but I climbed every one it was possible to climb, went into every cellar that it was possible to enter including the so called 'tunnel under the lakes' – all out of bounds, of course, but that was part of the fun.

My favourite was the Bourbon Tower which was a three storey tower which had been a cottage with a central 'chimney' but at that time had no floors! However, the stairs were built into the outside walls and conveniently someone had put a plank of wood between the top stairs and the central chimney! I visited it several times and 'walked that plank' without falling off!

My second favourite was Cobham Monument. The highest tower in the grounds although, in those days, the doorway was bricked up! However, there is a ledge about four metres up and just above someone had conveniently removed a block of stone so it was possible to crawl in! Just to prove that I got to the top, I took a photograph of Julian Lister and another boy called Miller (with both looking a little nervous!) I still love follies and today I have a small folly tower which I had built in a corner of my land a few years ago.

Another highlight of my life at Stowe was that I climbed the 'cedar' – once! This was a huge tree in sight of the school and 104' (30m+) high. It's strange to think now in these days of Health & Safety that no one ever stopped any of us from climbing it and some boys spent a lot of their free time up it too! It wasn't easy but I did have someone to guide me although I did my

The Bourbon Tower

best not to look down as we went up! Some of the more difficult parts had nicknames, including a wide branch which had no handholds at all! For some unknown reason this was known as 'Queen Caroline's c**t'. Why, I've no idea, but perhaps the person who named it knew something that we didn't! I got to the top!

A final memory was 'raiding' Tile House girls' boarding school which was situated just outside the school grounds! In my last year I got to know a boy called Dick Price who had a girlfriend there and he would, at a prearranged time, creep into the school grounds through the bushes and either wave at the girls or, if he was lucky, his girlfriend would briefly meet him outside. Of course expulsion would result if either of them were caught! He invited me to come with him which I did on two occasions.

Julian Lister and Miller at the top of Cobham Monument

However on the second, having just emerged from the bushes in front of the school, while we were busy waving to the girls who'd assembled in their common room, I felt a hand on my shoulder and a male voice behind me saying "what have we here?"! I shouted, "run Dick", then ducked down and ran as if my life depended on it! I remember diving headfirst over a five-bar gate, somersaulting to the other side and running all the way back to Stowe! Well, we both made it but it was a 'close thing' so I never went back!

> **Postscript**: In 1981 when I was in the States, I managed to track down my long-lost cousin, Tony Mackenzie, the 4th Baronet of Glenmuick. Following his education at Stowe, Tony emigrated to Canada. For a while he became a Canadian 'Mountie' before retiring to run a riding school on Vancouver Island with his Canadian wife, Marjorie. He was a most delightful man and always dressed in suit and tie with a white shirt and a stiff collar in the manner of an old-fashioned English gentleman. He and his wife Marjorie were both charming and hospitable. We talked about Stowe. He told me that after he'd had his time there, he considered himself a failure and consequently left Britain never to return! I understood exactly how he felt.

Guy's cousin Tony Mackenzie 4th Baronet of Glenmuick (in tailored suit, tie and stiff white collar) pictured on his 50th Wedding Anniversary with his wife Marjorie on his right. Others in the photograph are not clearly identified as Tony's description describes them as: "friend's wife" on his left, "friend" on his second right and "friend's wife's mother" on his far right. No risk of breaching Data Protection regulations there then!

Chapter 5
Applegarth and Freedom, 1963 – 1964

IT HAD BECOME quite obvious by mid-1963 that the teaching at Stowe, and probably my lack of application, would not result in me getting any A levels there, so my parents generously sent me to Applegarth which was a private College which literally "crammed" a two year A level course into one year!

Applegarth was a large house, almost next to Charterhouse School, and had a good reputation for getting results. It was a friendly environment and we had freedom (at last!) to go outside the school grounds and I enjoyed my year there. The teaching was, in the main, very good and, in the case of the English teacher, inspirational. Thanks to him, (and to my mother) I gained the love of English (and Scottish) literature and which I still have…

After a term, my friend, Martin "Thumbs" Bellamy joined me there and our occasional treat was to walk into Godalming and into the nearest pub where we'd each have a bottle of Brown ale and a packet of crisps! I recall that the Brown was 1/3p and the crisps 6d (less than 10p in total today!).

Although I hadn't played football at Stowe (it wasn't a football school!) because of my enthusiasm of the game, I became Captain of football (well, there were only about 25 of us in the whole school!) and we had some success playing matches against the Charterhouse houses which I really enjoyed.

I was also able to pursue my love of music as The Beat Club had just opened in Godalming. By chance we were just about the first to know about it and got complimentary memberships. We saw a band called Shorty and Them who had just recorded the Bo Diddley number *Pills* – "As I was laying in a hospital bed, a rock n roll nurse came to my head, she said hold out your hand and put out your tongue, I've got pills and I'll give you some…" etc, etc. I still play my drums along to this great number, written by one of my favourite artists, with the "hi-fi high" and our dogs asleep on the sofa curled up against Sally reading her book. How she can "switch off" with that level of noise is beyond me!

I also saw The Undertakers there. A fabulous band from Liverpool they came on stage appropriately dressed and with a coffin! They had just released their hit *Just a Little Bit* and are still performing today with, sadly, several enforced changes to their line-up.

During my time there I became, for a while, very friendly with a young, attractive trainee cook at Charterhouse. She and I spent quite a few evenings in "close contact" on a quiet dimly lit footpath which connected that school to the road to Godalming. Occasionally someone would venture past us with a smile and an apology. Golden days – or do I really mean, "dark evenings"!

I was very happy at Applegarth. It really was a breath of fresh air after Stowe, actually more of a storm! and I made several new friends. One was from Thailand and I recall him showing me a picture of his house there, which looked like a huge office block. In my amazement and, without thinking, I actually said that, but I don't remember him being impressed!

I also became friendly with someone I'll refer to as CM, who was set on becoming a priest. After we both left, we kept in touch and following my move to London, sometime later, he invited me out to dinner in a restaurant in Soho. So far so good! But what I didn't realise was that it was a gay (still illegal at that time!) restaurant! I never saw him again but realised that he'd not only found his calling but also his lifestyle too.

Robert Charles Austin Whittaker, Guy's Applegarth school friend who he always called 'Bob'. Pictured at a party in London during the 1960s

Robert Whittaker, although small in stature, was a huge character. I used to call him Bob although he'd always take pains to remind me that his name was "Robert Charles Austin" not Bob! When he was at Applegarth he had a strong Yorkshire accent although he was in fact from Wolverton (near Milton Keynes) which was absolutely fine. Later, when he moved to Dorset, where I occasionally saw him, his accent was broad Dorsetshire! He was very much a countryman, loved all country sports especially horse racing. For a short while his enthusiasm rubbed off on me until I told my father – who I thought would be pleased. He wasn't and begged me not to get involved in the "Geegees" as the sport had cost him so much over the years. So, as a consequence, I stopped.

While at Applegarth, Bob and I also decided to try and make some money in the afternoons and so we canvassed ourselves as "dog walkers" at 3/- (15p) per hour! This was, I suppose, my first business venture and we had quite a few customers. Our first canine client was called Copper, as I recall, a beautiful and well behaved Labrador type dog who we used to enjoy taking for walks.

Bob was convinced that he was always right. However, after several arguments with the headmaster (I can't remember what about!) Bob called the Head a f*****g c**t to his face, no doubt, jabbing him with his forefinger in the chest as he did so! Of course, this resulted in him being expelled! Bob's father was furious and came and collected him, but all the way home Bob kept telling his father he was in the right! In fact, the last time I spoke to Bob about this, many years later, he still insisted that he was right and the headmaster was a f*****g c**t!

Robert remained a friend until his very sad death from MS nearly 20 years ago. In his last years being able to only move his head and one arm he was looked after by his devoted, but long suffering, Filipino wife. She had come into his life after he refused to marry his long term girlfriend who then promptly went and married someone else.

If I'm in Dorset I always visit his grave and there are always fresh flowers on it left, I'm sure, by his ex-girlfriend.

Despite the excellent teaching at Applegarth I had no more success with my A levels there than I would have had at Stowe. Nor, as I recall, did Thumbs. It was huge disappointment not only for me but also for my parents as money was becoming an issue for them. Apart from education – in my case money largely wasted! – there was also the "money pit" that was Calgary House (and still is as Sally and I discovered when we tried to buy it a several years ago!) but, more significantly, the financial mismanagement by a dishonest stockbroker who'd been recommended to them!

So my next step was to get a job and relieve my parents of the financial responsibility of me! They'd done everything they possibly could for me and, apart from the lack of academic success and the negatives of Stowe (which stayed with me for years until I'd become an elected local Politician in Cornwall, many years later) there had been, over the years, some real positives too! So onwards, upwards and onto the Buckingham Labour Exchange.

The group picture taken by Guy (excluding Martin Bellamy who didn't want to be included) with the "English girl" standing 5th right

The "English Girl" photographed by Guy – in '60's David Bailey mode!

The "English Girl" pictured with Guy... her Knight in Shining Armour!

A kiss on the lips can be so continental but was she looking for a "diamond"? Whatever, Guy soon lost touch after this delightful romantic interlude

Chapter 6
School's Out and the Road to London, 1964

I LEFT SCHOOL in summer 1964 with no qualifications despite having had one year at Applegarth college, having failed Maths and French O level 5 times, with no idea of what sort of career I wanted, other than a desire to earn some money.

Rather than going home to the Isle of Mull, I moved in with my elderly cousins, Ethel and Madge Logan, who had a cottage near Buckingham and had so very kindly and generously provided me with a "home from home" while I was at Stowe.

So almost immediately I was off to the Labour Exchange in Buckingham where I got my first job on a farm, near Buckingham, for a period of 4 weeks to help with the harvest. I had to live in as the working days were long and I was on the princely sum of about 3/6 (18p.) an hour. Of course there was no room in the farmhouse (or maybe they didn't want me there) so I was put in a modern cottage nearby. It had no furniture other than a bed and a chair and no TV back in those days!

It was really hard work and my fellow worker who basically I got on well with, most of the time, liked to let me know how tough he was compared to me. He was appropriately known as "Digger". On my very first day, the farm owner asked me if I could drive a tractor. I immediately said "yes" as I had just passed my driving test (on Mull!) although I'd never driven one! He asked me to drive one of his down to a field to maybe try me out. Not realising that putting one's foot on the brakes was not the way to stop a tractor, I came charging up to the field, slammed my foot on the brakes and, of course, the tractor went sailing through the field gate. It was new one too! So, not a very auspicious start!

My life over these weeks seemed to follow a similar pattern, getting tractors stuck more than once in the silage pit etc. However, Digger and I did have a few fun evenings at the local pub where for the first and only time in my life I managed to drink 6 pints of bitter. Digger did slightly resent me as the long hours I had to put in resulted in me earning slightly more than his 10gns (£10.50p) pw fixed wage. We also had one or two arguments where he threatened to beat me up. He didn't as I told him I'd learnt Karate at school. I hadn't!

On one memorable (?) occasion I entered the farmhouse unexpectedly one afternoon and heard some unusual sounds coming from upstairs. Sort of moanings and a yelp or two! Then the farmer's wife and her brother-in-law came down the stairs doing up their clothes but didn't expect to see me in the kitchen! She demanded to know what was I doing there and I mumbled something and was ordered back to work! As I walked out I heard them discussing whether I'd heard anything. I never said anything, apart from discussing the incident with Digger, but the farmer's wife did seem to be a bit more friendly with me from then on!

Perhaps she'd been wondering if I'd "rat on her?" but, of course, I never did.

When my four weeks were up, the farmer halfheartedly offered me a few more weeks. It was an offer I was happy to refuse. Apart from anything else, my hands were in ribbons from lifting bales of hay as I never wore gloves, simply because I wanted to appear tough in front of Digger!

In any case, my parents had arranged for me to go to France for 3 weeks to work on the Vendage (grape harvest) in the hope that I might learn some French! And my school friend, Martin "Thumbs" Bellamy (whose mother felt the same for him) was lined up to join me.

So Thumbs and I, before having about a week's holiday in Mull, decided to have a look round the Soho music shops to kit ourselves out so we could one day hit the road as musicians! I bought a second-hand Broadway drum kit for £18 and Martin bought a 10 Watt Bird Amp and a Futurama 3 guitar (also second hand combined price £25) because they were the cheapest we could find! Plus, of course, a Chuck Berry songbook!

Sadly our best attempts at *Johnny B. Goode* and *Whole Lotta Shakin'* in Mull and later at his home in Gloucestershire were met with, at best, amused apathy, simply because nobody, including us, could recognise them! And then, after our brief holiday in Mull, we were off on our adventure.

I don't think anything really prepared us for our time near Dijon. Long before the EEU, life in the French countryside was primitive to say the least! In fact in the whole village there were only 2 flushing loos and when we arrived after many hours of travel, Martin asked: "Ou est le sale de bains?" (where is the bathroom?), everyone fell about laughing as there were no bathrooms in the village. A bath was standing in the yard in your swimmies and getting someone to hose you down!

We were in the biggest house in the village along with around 10 other students of different nationalities and along with everyone else we shared one hole in the ground in the yard. Needless to say with the summer heat, it absolutely stank! However our house did have one of the two flushing loos but only the women in our household were allowed to use it!

As far as learning French, it was a good experience as almost no one, apart from Thumbs and an English girl who was running away from a broken relationship spoke anything other than French. She was rather off-hand with us as she seemed to prefer fraternising with the locals.

All went well for a few days. Lunches were long and really quite good with copious amounts of red wine, even if some of the meat had a peculiar flavour and texture! Then we witnessed the most incredible cruelty to a small defenceless animal which resulted in the English girl going into hysterics. The more she cried the more the others mocked her! Of course, and despite her previous coolness to us, Thumbs and I sprang to her defence. We'd had to fight just to survive at Stowe so fighting, even against overwhelming odds was second nature to us, so we rolled up our sleeves and threatened to take on everyone! If the farmer hadn't intervened, this story might never have proceeded further, fortunately he did! He made all the others apologise and promise not to do anything like that again. An uneasy truce was called and an international incident was averted. Rather sadly, I was left with a deeply unfavourable impression and, as a result, I did not return to France for nearly 40 years.

Later, that evening after copious amounts of red wine and something a little stronger too, the matter was put behind us, and life in the vines carried on. Maybe, having seen me as something of a Knight in Shining Armour, a close friendship between the English girl and I commenced. However, one day, the farmer caught us canoodling (rather innocently) in the vines and sacked me on the spot! I immediately called my loyal friend, Thumbs, and said I've been sacked and we're both leaving! We went back to the farmhouse and started packing our things but probably because, at this critical time, part of his workforce was leaving the farmer called us back. I recall him saying "mal a tete" and tapping his head which we understood to be an apology (maybe he was jealous of me?) which we accepted and returned to work. We both then returned to England, filthy and smelly (!) vowing never to return.

As a postscript, I did meet the girl again in London, where she lived, but sadly the magic which we'd started to create in the vines had evaporated...

By now, my parents were becoming concerned about me getting a career. I took my army test and failed due to my flat feet. Despite the fact that I'd have to work my way up through the ranks due to my lack of A levels this was a disappointment to my father who had retired as a full Colonel.

So, I returned to my cousins' house and went back to the Labour Exchange. I immediately got a job in Richardson's paint factory in Buckingham as a "filler in" doing the job of anyone who didn't turn up for work. I actually enjoyed the job and even got myself a room at a pub in the town, as I had no transport.

I had several mates at the factory including Mick who was especially noticeable as he had the words "Cut Here" tattooed across his throat! He looked tough and probably was but we got on well and along with a couple of others used to go pubbing on pay day evening. The pub rules, where I was staying, were that, we lock the doors at 10.30 and you have to be in by then. Of course, one night I came back late, the doors were locked, so up the drainpipe I climbed, over a flat roof and up another and eventually got into my bedroom without anyone waking up. The next morning when I appeared for breakfast, I was met with stony glares and prolonged silence and the landlord demanded to know how I'd got in when he'd deliberately locked me out! Needless to say, he evicted me on the spot! So I went back to my cousins' house and an early bus ride to work. Actually this didn't last long as a lunchtime drinking session with my mates and a late return to work resulted in me being, well, given my cards (sacked) on the spot as I was perceived to be the ringleader – no one else got the sack. It just wasn't fair... boohoo!

While I was working at Richardson's paint factory, the 1964 General Election was held and who was the Labour Candidate for Buckingham? Well, none other than millionaire Robert Maxwell. Maxwell is now remembered without much affection for plundering the pension funds of the Mirror Group newspapers to shore up his businesses and save them from collapse! Those who are not as old as I may not be aware that the Conservative Government had by then been in power for some 13 years, the final ones dogged by some spectacular scandals! These included: the flight of spy, Kim Philby (the third man) in 1963, to the Soviet Union; the Christine Keeler affair which resulted in the resignation of Defence Minister, John Profumo (although many other prominent men were rumoured to have been involved) and, of course, the speculation that the "headless man" mentioned so prominently in the Argyll divorce case was, in fact, a Conservative Minister! Consequently, the country was clamouring for a change in government.

I recollect being one of a huge crowd in Buckingham Town Centre when Robert Maxwell made his victory address on the steps of the Town Hall, to an adoring throng following his victory over the Conservative candidate. In those days my politics were slightly to the left but, somehow, I felt that the Robert Maxwell who I saw and listened to on that day, somehow didn't ring true – yet, I never thought then that his business career would end the way it did. Nor for that matter (not that I was aware of her till many years later) that his adored daughter Ghislaine would one day end up being convicted of the appalling crime of "sex trafficking" young girls!

By this time, Mick had a new girlfriend who made it obvious that she didn't like me. Maybe she thought I was a bad influence on him? But one excursion we did make together was to a tattooist who I watched covering over Mick's throat tattoo with a butterfly – maybe he really was tough as he never flinched!

I then got a job concreting the bases of electricity pylons, in November/December which was miserable and very cold and the Polish workers referred to me as "the boy". I remember drinking tea from an empty tin and them complaining that I couldn't work fast enough. We were on piece work and earning £25 per week, a huge amount in those days! So once again, I got the sack but I had saved nearly £100 in those 4 weeks!

Postscript: I think its fair to state that by 1970, my politics had turned right of centre and I remember sitting up most of the Election night of that year listening to the radio in my bedsit and hearing the details of Conservative leader, Edward Heath's unexpected win! I also recall, while working in Lloyds of London when the new Chancellor, Anthony Barber, visited which resulted in huge applause by the brokers and underwriters present on that day. These events helped kick-start my lifelong interest in politics but, as far as Local Government is concerned, I've always stood, and been elected, as an Independent – not beholden to any political party.

Chapter 7
London at Last, 1965

JUST BEFORE I left Buckingham, I had an interview for a proper job as a trainee building supervisor with Limmer & Trinidad Lake Asphalt Co. Hooray! I got the job at the amazing salary of £9 per week and started work at their Island Row depot which was at the wrong end of Commercial Road, East London.

The company arranged digs for me which turned out to be a house of bedsits just off Manor House, North London. Fortunately for me, one of my fellow trainees was living there and he even had a car, a minivan and for £1 per week he agreed to take me back and forth each day. On reflection, this was almost the worst place I've ever lived as it was gloomy and poorly maintained. Worst of all in the six months I lived there, I only remember meeting one other resident. All the others seemed to like to be anonymous as when I either came in or walked out of my room, doors seemed to close! But it was cheap, just £2.10/- (£2.50) per week! My parents knowing my financial situation insisted on giving me an allowance of £10 per month which I did my best to refuse and tried never to use, simply because I was determined to make it on my own. However, I did use a small part of it to buy a winter coat! But, on the one occasion when my mother visited London, I wouldn't let her come and see my room, it certainly was depressing! Much later I found out that the block was owned by those notorious gangsters, the Krays.

There was no television in my room. In fact I didn't own a TV till the very late 1960s. My one real enjoyment was going to Finsbury Park and watching the Wrestling whenever I could afford the entrance fee, was it 5/-? It was fantastic entertainment and I enjoyed it so much that one evening I went and asked one of the doormen if I could have a word with Dale Martin, the promoter because I wondered if I could become a pro wrestler! He explained that the promoter wasn't there that night but asked me if I had any experience of fighting – of course my answer was "yes!". What I didn't tell him was that my skills were learnt at one of the top Public Schools as a means to survive! I missed the next week's show but, the following week, he saw me and told me that the promoter had been there the previous week and asked to meet me! I suppose, in hindsight, I wouldn't have lasted long with the likes of Mick McManus, Giant Haystacks and Adrian Street.

I quite enjoyed my work at Island Row, the other staff were both friendly and helpful but also used to take me out on roofing jobs to learn the business so I could become a Supervisor. I do recall having an argument with one elderly lady about who did most to win the War, Churchill or the men on the front line but apart from that and the unfortunate situation of me being blamed for letting a lorry crash into the Flooring Manager's car, the day before he went on holiday with it, all went really well.

One memorable time was when one of the Contracts Managers found himself with a crossed line (well, the telephone system was like that then!) with some girls who worked in a hair salon nearby. He called me over and suggested that I talk to them. Which I did! They then invited me to come to the salon and meet them. Which I also did! After some chat they showed me the first real "porno" pictures I'd ever seen and asked me if I liked them! Of course as a young and somewhat naive 18 year old I didn't know what to say… so, after some thought, I said I didn't! Quite clearly this wasn't the answer they hoped for (I'd never experienced a twosome in those far off days, let alone a threesome!) and I was ushered out of the salon quite soon afterwards. Perhaps, once again, if things had worked out as the girls had intended (?), I would now have a story to tell! Heigh Ho…

All the trainees from all over the UK occasionally were brought to the Fulham depot for intense training. At one of these sessions, there was the most annoying fellow trainee who kept interrupting the trainer and seemed to know more than he did! His name? Martin Kennedy-Bell who later became, and still is, one of my best and most loyal friends.

Anyway and back to my job, after my 6 month initial training had completed, I was told that I needed an extra 3 months training (maybe the crashed car didn't help?) and was transferred to the Southampton Depot just outside the city. I also got a salary increase to £10 per week, a rise of over 10% so I was able to tell my parents that the allowance they had insisted on, was no longer needed!

Chapter 8

Southampton calling, 1965 – 1966

I ARRIVED AT Limmer and Trinidad's depot at Chandlers Ford, met some of the staff there and was taken to the Company "digs" which was a terraced house in Cranberry Avenue, Southampton. However, no one warned me that this was, at that time, right in the middle of Southampton's red light district! Did the company realise, I wonder? The Street Offences act was in its infancy, so there was no shortage of "talent" – which is perhaps not always an accurate description! on display – but, certainly something of an eye opener for a shy lad from a sheltered background.

I enjoyed my first few months with the company and it was a beautiful part of the Country too. Also, as my father knew the Rosthchild family from his racing days, I was invited to their beautiful Estate and they were charming and hospitable! Although they offered to come and collect me and take me back, I always insisted on getting the bus. When they rang me, they had to ring the office as there was no phone in Cranberry Avenue – this did cause some raised eyebrows in the office that a junior like me, on £10 per week could know a family like that!

While in Southampton, I sold the Velocette 350cc motorcycle I had bought in London and ridden down on for the sum of £2.50 (it had cost me £15) and the next day the buyer came and asked for his money back. I refused! But I then bought a BSA 500cc Shooting Star for £28 which I absolutely loved. I wore my leathers and visited the "ton-up caff"! Great fun too! I also recall riding up to Martin's home near Cirencester in Gloucestershire in the pouring rain! By the time I got there none of my lights were working (well it was a British bike!) but thankfully the electrics had dried out overnight so I was able to return safely. I also remember taking one of my fellow trainees on the pillion to Bournemouth on a sunny day! Being a British bike, its stopping power was poor and when a small sports car stopped suddenly in front of me, I went into its back-end and we both ended up sitting in the road. When we had all dusted ourselves down and found that nothing was damaged including the sports car and ourselves, we continued on our journey. My passenger seemed more nervous after that and when we arrived he said that he'd never go on the back of my bike again! He never even thanked me for the lift and he even got the bus back to Southampton!

Prior to leaving the next year, I sold it for £58 – so my early vehicle dealing wasn't entirely unprofitable. The prices for these bikes today? The Velo maybe £2.5K and the Beezer maybe £4K . Who could have imagined they would ever reach such incredible prices back in 1966!

After a few months, I was promoted to a Junior Supervisor on the felt roofing division at a salary of £12 per week. I also got a company car, a Vauxhall Viva!

Some months after getting it, I got a bit over enthusiastic going round a corner and ended up sitting on the inside of the roof. The car had flipped over and there were no seat belts in those days! I wasn't hurt at all but the car was a write-off. The company weren't very happy and warned me that another write-off would result in my career getting similar treatment! More annoyingly for me was that I needed it for a new "date" I had lined up that weekend. In those far off days a car wasn't just for transport.

Basically, I enjoyed my job and got on well with the tradesmen who worked for the company mainly on "piece rate" and some made a lot of money! I remember having a discussion with one who was complaining about his wages and so I said, have a look at my wage slip! He did and said: "That's not bad for a weekly wage". I did, however, have to point out that that was my calendar monthly wage. He couldn't believe it as he was earning over 3 times as much as me! Even at that time I was starting to wonder how long it would take and how high I would have to get in the company to actually start making some real money!

I may have got on with the tradesmen well but after a few weeks another trainee moved into the digs. He was a fellow Scot (but with a Scottish accent!) and from day one, he and I just didn't get on! We kept chipping away at each other till the day came that we had no option but to fight (well, the clans always fought each other when there were no English to fight – just to keep in practice!) We walked down to an area of waste land nearby and battle commenced! We fought the good fight for a while then, almost in unison, we decided enough was enough and called it a day and shook hands. I always considered that if there was a winner on that day, it was me! When we returned to our digs somewhat bruised and bloodied we both said that we'd had an accident although I'm not sure that anyone believed us! But, from that moment on, we became firm friends and remained as such till we both went our separate ways.

Finding myself with evenings to spare and not being used to watching the TV that these digs had, with programmes chosen by a majority decision, I decided to put an advert in the local paper which stated: "Drummer seeks group or musician to form one". As a result I met Bill and Bob and joined their band. The Blue Stars. Yes, they really did name themselves after the then well known chain of garages! Fortunately for me, Bill was not only a brilliant guitarist, bass player and singer but drummer too! I really didn't have much of a clue about drumming then! He didn't quite teach me all I know but he gave me a good start! I'm eternally grateful to him for helping set me on course for what became my most important lifetime hobby, collecting guitars. I kept in

THE BLUE STARS

★

B. GEDDES
5, VINE ROAD,
COXFORD,
SOUTHAMPTON

VOCAL AND
INSTRUMENTAL
GROUP

touch with both of them until Bill's untimely death a few years ago. Later both his daughter and granddaughter made contact with me via my website and social media.

We did some gigs too, starting off at the Railway Inn, Eastleigh in 1965 at the sum of £6! But, in 1966, we played possibly the biggest venue I've ever played at, The Southampton Guildhall on a 60s package show! Since then and with the help of social media, I've actually made contact with other musicians on that same bill (see the Background page on the Guitar Collection website)!

> FRIDAY AUGUST 5
> **DANCE**
> at
> **Soton Guildhall**
> to
> THE NITE PEOPLE
> LES FLEUR DE LYS
> THE FOOTPRINTS
> and introducing
> THE BLUE STARS
> Full Refreshments
> Doors open 7.30.

However after about 15 months in Southampton, the company decided that I should be transferred to Newcastle (but without my company car!) and this double whammy was a step too far for me so I decided to get a job back in London and became a trainee Lloyds Insurance broker in late 1966. Surely there was a better financial future for me both in London and in The City!

The Blue Stars

The Hon. Victoria Baillie and Mr. Guy Mackenzie.

For two years running Guy was invited to the Royal Caledonian Ball and on one occasion his picture appeared in *Tatler* magazine

Chapter 9
London Again, 1966 – 1971

MY LIFE IN LONDON started with me living in Fulham SW6 as my Southampton Limmer & Trinidad manager's wife's parents had a house with a small flatlet which they let out there. I had to get to the City everyday by the Underground from Parsons Green to Monument as my new employers, Bland Welch, were based in Fenchurch Street. My memories of the Underground are of the overcrowding in rush hour, the intense heat in summer and always having wet legs till my trousers dried when it rained.

Some of my insurance policies today are still with companies which evolved from that job but I can honestly say that the next 2 years of working life were the most boring and miserable that I've ever experienced. I had to learn the business and I just kept dreaming of getting into Lloyds and the untold riches that would result, once I understood insurance!

Well, it was a dream, but Lloyds did turn out to be pivotal in my career and, surprisingly, in my life too.

Why was it boring? Well, insurance is boring! Why was it miserable? Well, you try working in a huge open plan office which had windows down one side only and who sat under the windows? In those days before computers, it was the typists and they always dressed in the thinnest of clothes and were always, seemingly, cold! Whilst the men, sat on the inside and had to always wear suits! In summer it was unbearably hot and whenever I tried to open the windows, the typists would close them saying they were cold!

It got to the stage that several of them refused to speak to me. Well I guess they were bored too. Endless typing must be boring! This really got to me for a while especially as they went out of their way to be friendly to others – glaring at me as they did so!

However over a period of time, I devised a strategy to deal with this. I would be extra friendly and pretend that I didn't care! This did throw them off course and gradually, when they believed that their persecution had no effect on me this time, they got back to speaking to me but – it has to be said – with no real enthusiasm!

It wasn't all bad. Martin Kennedy-Bell had followed me to Southampton, but lived elsewhere as, by then, Limmer & Trinidad had decided that the red light district wasn't the place for their trainees! Martin had now gone into insurance too with "The Pru" (The Prudential), and he was based at their huge headquarters in the City. He was courting at the time but I used to see him for lunch. The Pru had a fantastic subsidised canteen and he used to say to me: "Come and have lunch, they'll never know you don't work for the Pru," and they never did!

After about six months in Fulham, Martin Bellamy moved up to London and we got a flat in Emperor's Gate SW7. It was in this same road that a similar sized flat became the home, in her sad later years, of the 1960's pop sensation, the singer Kathy Kirby. Our underground station was Gloucester Road. Great postcode, shame about the flat! A run down, one bedroom flat and we had to have someone else share it with us so we could afford the rent. I drew the short (or was it the long?) straw and slept in the living room where at least I could "entertain" on my own! and they shared the bedroom.

It wasn't the happiest time in my life as I got in with a very wealthy set, drank too much, got into debt and found out my first real girlfriend, as it turned out, preferred the company of a young, good looking South African man. Devastating for me at the time but part of life's rich tapestry. The last thing I heard was the distant sound of wedding bells in South Africa. I hope they've had a happy life!

Life wasn't all bad or sad, as I was invited once to Queen Charlotte's Debutante's Ball then two years running to the Royal Caledonian Ball and although I'm no dancer, I love the sound of Scottish music and the Bagpipes and I got my picture in *Tatler* magazine too!

However, after one major drinking session, I had a serious car accident and wrote off my much cherished Minivan and very nearly myself. I'd bought it for £134 and it was only insured for third party risks. My two fellow travellers some how escaped serious injury but I was unconscious for 4 hours and my sight was at risk for several weeks having gone headfirst through the windscreen into a stationary lorry. Sometime later, my kind mother generously sold some jewellery and bought me a second-hand Triumph Herald. I didn't refuse the offer of financial help –thank you Mother!

This incident become a turning point in my life for several reasons. I was off sick for several weeks and on full pay too which helped get me out of debt. This gave me a chance to reassess my lifestyle and start to turn things around. Whilst in hospital, neither of my fellow travellers in the van bothered to come and see me although Martin Bellamy, as I remember, came every day – so much for transitory friendship! I never got into debt again (even to buy a car) except for investment purposes.

After a period at my cousins' house (sadly, they had both recently died), I was looked after by their kindly housekeeper, Mrs Marshall, I then went up to Mull. On my return, Bland Welch must have taken pity on me and my battered face still full of bits of windscreen (the hospital Doctors had helpfully said: "You'll have to let them work their own way out") and promoted me to the position of Junior Broker in Lloyds at the vast salary of £1,000 p.a.! My duties were what was known as a "scratchboy" which meant I got minor amendments to insurance policies – "scratched" by minor underwriters – and also to queue on behalf of the senior brokers waiting to see the "lead" underwriters. Sometimes the queues lasted for days so I had plenty of time to chat to fellow brokers and junior underwriters.

Lloyds was a melting pot of people and ideas with everyone (and it was men only then!!), seemingly, looking for an opportunity! Whatever you wanted or wanted to know, you just had to find the right person and that's how I got into Swipe!

Swipe was a domestic cleaning fluid although how much ended up with the consumer is open to debate! It was sold direct by an ingenious Multi Level marketing technique which has since been made illegal! I worked hard in my spare time for about 6 months, didn't make much money – who ever did, I wonder, apart from the people at the top!? – but it helped me to realise that I had an ability to sell. From then on I've always had to have a second business or hobby in my spare time, although I put my drumming on hold for a while.

One person who was looking for an opportunity was one of my bosses, Ray Mackender, who was a music impresario, talent spotter and manager. His most successful protégé was Mark Winter (*Venus in Blue Jeans* etc.) Mark is still performing today and I recently interviewed him for my YouTube channel. We discussed Ray who was a really helpful and friendly person but a victim of sexual discrimination. Ray's walk, his hand gestures, his flick of the hair were much mocked by one of his colleagues who I can still see now! Embarrassingly for us Junior Brokers, this happened right in front of us! Being gay was still almost illegal back then and discrimination rife against gay people. How times change and for the better too!

Another example was when my father found some Mackenzie odds and ends which he was going to throw away, but decided to send them to me offering to split anything I got 50/50 with him. He thought they weren't worth anything so, having asked around, I was directed to the one dealer in London specialising in such items. I sold them for £55. That doesn't seem a lot today, but my share was about a week and a half's net wages so I was delighted but more pleased that I'd done something for my father who was simply astounded and mentioned it to me several times!

Unfortunately with people looking for a opportunity there is always a dark side. Let me explain: I had an ex-Etonian friend called William (the name has been changed to protect the guilty!) whose father was one of the top people in Lloyds. For about a year we were level pegging and, I thought, good friends but he got his promotion before I did, and seemed on the way to the very top!

Having achieved this elevation and obviously feeling very important, he decided to ignore me and pretend he didn't know me as I was still a Junior! Annoying!

For a long time I never thought much more about it, but several years later, I saw William's picture and name splashed across the front pages of every newspaper! He had just been captured by Interpol as he was the front-man for a major international drugs ring! I could hardly believe it and so wrote to his father c/o Lloyds for confirmation. His father wrote a long letter back saying how disappointed he was but blamed his ex-wife for William's fall from grace (if that's what one calls serving time in Wormwood Scrubs!)

About the time I got into Swipe, I met Julie (her name has been changed to protect, in her case, the innocent) and we became a couple and remained so for some time. She helped develop my appreciation of the arts and culture, especially the West End plays such as *There's a Girl In my Soup* and Shakespeare. I loved *Macbeth* and always will remember a magical production of *Midsummer Night's Dream* in the Regents Park open air theatre. I still try to see this wonderful play every year. However, I hated the ballet and opera and still do. For me once was more than enough!!

On the rare occasions when I could afford to take Julie out for dinner, it was to either The Stock Pot, just off Knightsbridge which cost just over £1 for a freshly made Spaghetti Bolognaise and a glass of wine, The Bistro Vino at South Kensington where a paté starter, followed by steak, chips and peas plus a glass of wine cost about 35/- or, my favourite, The Trencherman, which was owned by actor Terence Stamp, which offered a huge main course for 2 plus a carafe of wine for just £3.

We also went once to the 555 café in Battersea Park Road made famous by Princess Margaret and her husband, the former Anthony Armstrong Jones. Inexpensive maybe, but somehow it didn't do it for us!

I'm getting ahead of myself now, but the first time that I started to believe that property was my future, was when Martin KB and I had decided to buy a large house together and rent out rooms. We actually found one in Munster Road, Fulham with 6 bedrooms for £6,500 – so 4 bedsits and one each for us – but no lender would advance more than 2 and a half times one salary (not two!) and neither of us could raise the difference so our ambitions, at this time, were thwarted.

This all happened at about the time that Julie's mother organised a 3 month trip for her in the States and presented it to Julie as a "fait accompli". Before she left and realising my disappointment over the house in Munster Road, Julie said that she'd buy one for me when she got back little understanding my personal ambitions and desire that, if I was going to make it, I'd make it on my own! Maybe it was that when we were apart, I realised her outlook and ambitions didn't match mine or perhaps it was her political affiliation, but when she got back, I'd moved on. Although the die had been cast, Julie remained in my thoughts for a long time afterwards. Perhaps her mother got her wish? I'll never know.

But I've digressed and now return to life just before Swipe…

After about a year, Martin Bellamy and I could no longer bear to live in the squalor of the flat we'd rented and went our separate ways. After two false starts, including moving into a rundown house in Chelsea – It was owned by a young film director and his wife who were friends of Andre Previn and film star Mia Farrow. I seemed to be the only one of the five of us who minded that the only shower in the house didn't work and there was no bath! – I then moved into a large bedsit on the top floor of a mansion block flat in Drayton Gardens. It had a lovely west view over the rooftops, I even had my own first TV, luxury indeed! I was happy there and stayed there until I bought my own flat.

Back in Lloyds in the days after Swipe, I too was looking for a new opportunity and it came in a surprising way! Queuing to see an underwriter in Lloyds, the broker next to me said he had a Vauxhall Cresta (yes one of the really big ones with American styling) that was worth £50 but would cost £75 to repair and didn't know what to do with it! Of course like any young person, I used to follow car prices and knew it had a value so I said I'd take it off his hands (for nothing!) which he agreed to provided that I came and collected it – which I did. I immediately advertised it in the *Evening Standard*, for £55, had a number of replies and sold it for £50. Well, it's hard to believe now, but in those far off days there was actually a shortage of cars to buy and the waiting list for a new one was often about 3 months!

And so my part time car dealing days started. I bought my next car from another queuing broker in Lloyds. It was a left hand drive Mk II Sunbeam Alpine. I paid £50 for it, drove it down to a car dealer I knew of in Fulham and sold it for £75!

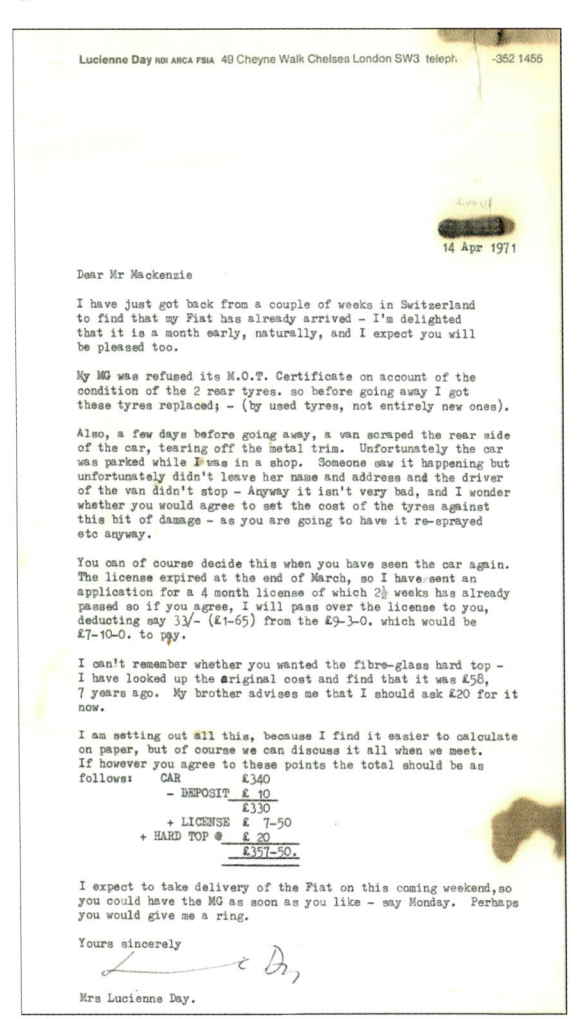

So then it was onwards and upwards but the best deal I did was on a battered, but almost new, MGB (which I'd been told about by the lads in the garage opposite) which was owned by Robin Day's (who was then a major TV interviewer) wife. So I went to see her and agreed a deal at £340 and I still have the paperwork! A few weeks later when her new car arrived, she contacted me by letter, but asked for another £20 for the hard top and £7.50 for the tax! I stuck to my guns and only agreed to pay for the unexpired car tax! Two days later I sold it for £480 to a friend of a friend and charged extra for the tax!

But not all of my deals were so easy, for example the back street garage which I sometimes used (they always liked to tell of their friendship with one of the ex-enforcers of the Krays – maybe to ensure that I paid my bills!) for inexpensive repairs had an

American Estate for sale at £240 which was a fair retail price, a Ford Fairlane as I recall. A few days later they phoned me and said they'd accept £180 provided I paid them immediately which I did! However although they let me have the log book, they kept coming up with excuses as to why I couldn't have the car, despite having paid them the money!

So I contacted Martin KB and asked him if he'd come with me to see them to try and get the car. In those days Martin could look sinister without trying… he wore tinted glasses, a very smart 3-piece pin striped suit, didn't smile very often and always had one hand in the upper pocket of his waistcoat! Quite clearly when we turned up at the garage, the two partners thought I had brought a gangster with me (with a "shooter" in his waistcoat pocket!) and nervously asked me, looking at Martin, what the problem was? When I said I'd come for the car they couldn't wait to give it to me! Problem solved! Thanks Martin!

People might ask today what did you do about road tax and insurance? No problem, as in those days, you just wrote "tax in post" on your windscreen and my car insurance covered me for driving other cars - I never registered any in my name! Life was, in some ways, much simpler then before computers! Maybe I was just lucky too!

But by now Martin KB and I had moved on to selling Unit Trusts which was a difficult sell but, we were surprised to discover years later that the exaggerated pay-outs predicted, actually weren't far off the mark – if one cashed in at the right time!

Thanks to the sale of cars in my spare time I had built up the deposit for a flat and, hearing from one of my contacts in Lloyds, that an "out of town" estate agents were selling ex Council flats in Central London below their real value, I contacted them immediately. The first flat I saw was a 2 bedroom flat in Asburnham Mansions, SW10 and the price? £5,150 which I could afford despite using up nearly all my savings! Only problem was that I had also used up my car trading working capital on the deposit and fees for my flat. And as Unit Trust sales were slowing down, I started selling typing courses, 2 or 3 evenings a week, to "leads" supplied by the Typing sales company. They were easy to sell as the customer paid £4 deposit (which was my sales commission), signed up and then was lent a typewriter for the duration of the course but how many typewriters were repatriated, I'll never know as I'd long gone by then! But I moved into my flat in 1971 and, knowing that I could sell it locally for more than the amount I'd paid, started looking around to see what I could afford. Well, I could get 2 conversion flats in Parsons Green for about £7,000 then - one I could buy outright and the other would have to be on mortgage. However my property ambitions would have to wait several years because events, which I'd never anticipated, suddenly overtook me and very soon my life changed forever, but that's another story…

Chapter 10
All Change! 1972

THE YEAR 1972 brought greater changes in my life than I could ever have imagined!

In 1971, I had bought my first property in Chelsea – well, in the "Worlds End" of SW10 anyway! Although I had no money, I owned a battered sports car so, in a way, I was almost "a man about town"! Seemingly just a few months later in 1972, I was a married man with a child on the way driving an elderly 4 door saloon car! Here's how it happened.

I'd met Paulene through a friend at Lloyds and, within a short space of time we married in February at Chelsea Register Office. Our reception was held at my cousin, Gilbert's (Lord Kilmarnock) beautiful Grosvenor Estates owned Belgravia home which had a ballroom in the back of the house. My best man was Martin Kennedy-Bell and my friend, Martin "Thumbs" Bellamy was also in attendance.

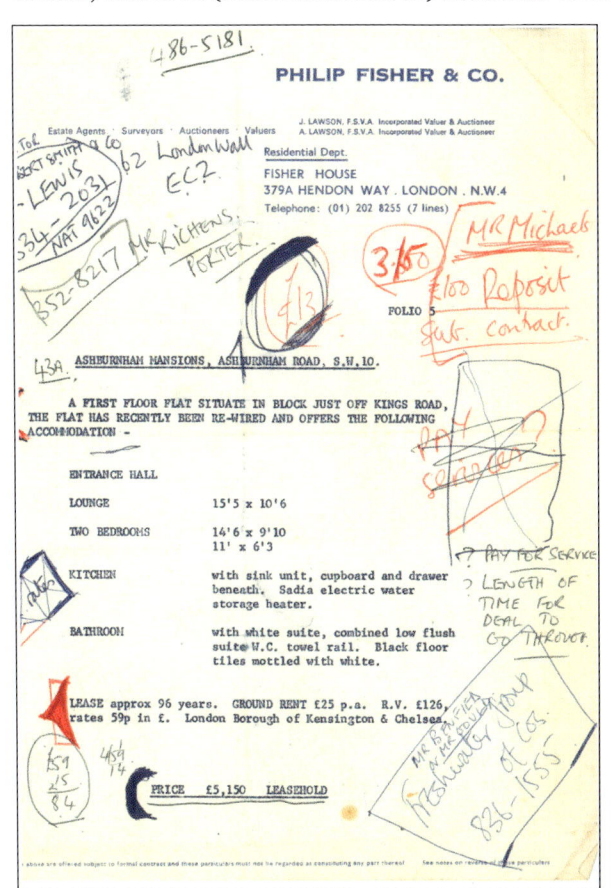

In those early days Paulene, under the strict and determined supervision of her mother, was a respected graphic artist. She supplemented her income with freelance design work in the evenings which she undertook in her mother's home near Park Royal, then about 15 minutes' drive away from my flat. She lived here until our marriage.

Amanda was born on the 19th May. Of course, she changed our lives forever. In June, about 6 weeks before his death, my father, looking very frail, made the trip to London and was delighted to meet his grandchild. I have always been happy to know that he met her as I knew how much it meant to him.

During the year, with Paulene's mother's help, the flat was redecorated. Paulene's flair for design transformed the living room into a space that all our visitors remarked upon. Despite the second-hand furniture, given to me by the caretaker of the flats where I previously lived this was to prove to be a brief glimpse of what might have been!

Paulene's mother also taught me to lay carpets which stood me in good stead when I first started, "on a shoestring", several years later, the property portfolio which Sally and I now own.

This was also the year that I moved out of London having allowed myself to be cajoled into buying an ultra-modern detached house in High Wycombe. It had been built by Sir Francis Dashwood whose ancestor was famous for founding the Hell Fire Club. The notorious 'goings on' of these 18th century high-society rakes took place in caves at West Wycombe which was only about a mile away and somewhere I enjoyed visiting!, together with the Dashwood Estate. The purchase was financed by the profit made on the flat which I sold for £11,750! I now had the responsibility of a wife and child so the time had come for a new career. The obvious option was as a salesman. Consequently, I got a job as a trainee sales representative with the Unilever Company, Clynol purveyors of ladies' hair-dressers' supplies, who just happened to also be based in High Wycombe. But I was still trading in old "bangers" to supplement my income!

After a rocky start, I was given my own territory and within 18 months had become the most successful salesman (of about 60) in the company. As a result of this achievement coupled with some "badgering" from me, I managed to get myself included in the Unilever management trainee scheme and became, the first non-University educated, ex-sales rep. ever to achieve this!

Chapter 11
Clynol, High Wycombe and Fat Man's Toy!
1972 – 1978

MY NEW HOUSE was situated on the outskirts of High Wycombe with fabulous views to the surrounding countryside through two huge picture windows which effectively took up an entire elevation. It had a double slope flat roof but almost no insulation. While it was warm in winter with its warm air central heating, in summer it was like a greenhouse! It had a "pocket handkerchief" of a front garden and the back was even smaller! With the road in front serving the whole estate, it was actually like living in a goldfish bowl! Every car that passed seemed to want to have a look in. There were only 3 TV stations back then so this activity provided something of a local, upmarket version of *Coronation Street* but with a modern twist! Consequently, within just over 3 years we were to move on.

Clynol, was a division of Unilever, a huge conglomerate which manufactured shampoo, hairspray etc. In those days it was based just a mile away. I was initially given a couple of weeks training with a successful sales rep who explained to me how to deal with the hairdressers who were our customers. Clynol was an old-fashioned supplier of ladies hairdressing products which lagged behind the market leaders Wella and L'Oreal and relied on promotions to maximise the product sales, rather than national advertising. Often there were offers like: "Buy 4 gallons of shampoo and get one free". As the years went on, the promotions got more generous – sometimes, "buy 1 get 1 free!" Or buy so many and get a free gift – which was very effective with some salon managers!

But my trainer had a twist on this which he confided to me. If a salon is delivered a product by mistake (which happened quite often!) or over ordered (not unusual!) just offer to take the unwanted product back yourself. Send a memo to head office authorising a refund but don't bother to send the product back to head office as, the chances are, they'll forget about it even if they contacted you asking for it to be returned. This will give you the option to either make up your own offers or sell it for cash!

I couldn't quite see the logic in this for the company! I did occasionally take his advice as the company was so inefficient, but I never was stupid enough to sell any product for cash as this would obviously result in dismissal if discovered! Needless to say, about a year later my "trainer" was dismissed, no doubt for that very reason!

When the company considered that I was trained sufficiently to be given my own territory, it just happened to be the one based on a 50 or so mile radius of the Clynol Head Office in High Wycombe!

I initially struggled to achieve my monthly sales targets and this resulted in me being somewhere very close to the bottom of the entire company sales force of about 60 which put my future prospects with the company in some doubt! So I decided to change tack… and my secret? You'll have to wait for the sales training video on my YouTube channel! Coming soon! It was legal and it worked so, within a matter of 3 months, I was top sales representative in the whole company!

To begin with the Sales Director didn't believe my figures thinking wrongly, of course, that I was emulating my trainer whose career had just hit the buffers! However, when the company realised that my results were genuine, I became something of a star. I was feted with commission which was actually very modest! but, more importantly it improved my future prospects with the Sales Management team and the Company Director.

Quite early on, I'd realised that progression and life in Clynol, or any company, as a salesman was relentless as one was only as good as the previous months' results. In Clynol and Unilever as a whole, the way to the top was via the Management Trainee scheme. The scheme was specifically reserved for University graduates and was via "Marketing" – the profitable promotion of a business or service. So I resolved to try and doorstep my way into the Marketing Department at the earliest possible opportunity.

The opportunity came in 1974, when one of three graduate trainees left and, on the basis of my sales results (and natural intelligence !?!?) I somehow managed to get myself promoted to Junior Product Manager. My two remaining colleagues were a little suspicious of me as I wasn't a university graduate like them. They kept referring to the "stumblebums" which was their not too flattering description of the salesmen! Well, we were in competition, after all! But I largely ignored them hoping they'd go away. In due course one did and life was a lot easier with her replacement. He and the other member of the "team" didn't like each other from day one!

Clynol taught me time management, as a salesman. As a "marketing man" I learnt all about business profitability, how to construct and cost marketing proposals, also public speaking which served me well when I became an elected local politician many years later. Bland Welch along with Clynol were both pivotal in my life.

Financially life was quite tough. My mortgage, although only £7,000, was at the limit of what I could afford despite the car sales. These were becoming more challenging as the Japanese imports flooded in and car buyers became more "street wise"! As a consequence, going out was really a nonstarter, especially as Paulene's "get up and go" had unfortunately stayed in London. Consequently, holidays were almost always at my mother's house. An early holiday at Calgary proved too much for Paulene when Iona, the Duchess of Argyle called in unexpectedly!

Iona was the daughter-in-law of my father's one time friend, Ian Campbell the 11th Duke of Argyle whose divorce from his wife Margaret (Iona's predecessor) in 1963 had scandalised the nation. The divorce case of Argyll v Argyll was infamous resulting is a huge amount of newspaper coverage. The whole affair put the House of Argyle in deep disgrace, neither Margaret, condemned as a nymphomaniac, nor Ian seen as violent man who essentially married for money to support his various enterprises and estates, came out of it well! It had been Margaret and her money that had enabled the restoration of Inveraray Castle. In 2021 the story was made into the television drama *A Very British Scandal* staring Claire Foy as Margaret and Paul Bettany as the Duke.

My father was appalled by the whole sorry business, particularly as his former friend had sold his story to the newspapers. Times change! and I suspect had it all happened today, Margaret, who was very much a free spirit, would be regarded rather differently, at least by the general public. I regard myself as fortunate to have met Margaret – regarded as a great beauty in her heyday – when I was a lad of 7 or 8. I found her charming and quite unlike the way she was portrayed in the newspapers after the divorce.

When Paulene met Iona she looked at her as if she'd seen a ghost. She visibly shook when introduced and grabbed Amanda for comfort, hugging her to her body as she sidled into a corner of the drawing room, unable to speak! It was so embarrassing, not just for me, but for Iona too and she left soon after, somewhat nonplussed and never to return! It didn't bode well for the future.

The reality was that Paulene was disinclined towards fresh air, exercise and Highland weather! Sadly we had little in common apart from our deep love for our daughter Amanda. We came from different worlds and stepping up to a part of mine was simply beyond her capabilities.

My mother sold Calgary in 1976 and, after she moved to Norfolk, we holidayed with her there too, apart from once in Cornwall. This holiday introduced me to a part of the country which I immediately fell in love with and where, several years later, I would make my home.

Back in the early 1970s, after several months of endlessly watching, mainly boring, evening TV, I decided to try and find another band to eventually supplement my earnings with income from gigs which I'd had a taste of in Southampton. Looking through the local paper one weekend, I saw an advert which immediately caught my eye which started: "Are you middle aged but still alive…" and ended "…drummer wanted". Well, I did feel somewhat middle aged but, I was very much still alive and joined Jack and Dennis who had been trying to put a band together for several years without success.

After about 6 months of practice, fuelled by home brewed beer and calling ourselves "Fat Man's Toy", we were ready for our first gig – in the function room of a pub in Reading. We looked forward to it with anticipation. When the evening came we arrived early full of excitement! But, as we set up our equipment, there was an eerie silence in the room which endured throughout the evening and, in fact, we always outnumbered our audience! The evening was a disaster! But we did get paid!

We almost broke up but decided to practice even harder as we were determined

The Earthborn line up was (left to right): Mike Pusey, lead guitar & vocals; Guy Mackenzie, drums and vocals; Eric, lead vocals and guitar and Dennis Mitchell on bass guitar

to succeed. Luckily Jack lived in a detached bungalow so noise wasn't an issue with his neighbours and his kitchen gave us enough room to set up our equipment. However, the one victim of our music was Jack's treasured crystal glass collection which was displayed on a shelf! After one "all out" practice session, no doubt we played lots of Status Quo numbers, the shelf parted company with the wall which it was attached to! The result - just a pile of broken glass! Ouch!

Apart from playing drums my job was to find bookings and, after a few weeks, with several in our diary, we hit the road again. This time we were a success and ended up doing between 1 and 2 gigs every weekend. We even played at the Bell in Maidenhead which was a well-known local venue. I have the recording, done on a £10 cassette tape recorder, of me on lead vocals, and playing drums, on the Eddie Cochran number, *Twenty Flight Rock*. This recording is now on YouTube!

Over time, as it always seems to be with bands, personalities and content get in the way and the band split. Surprisingly, Dennis wanted to leave his long-term friend, Jack, and decided to stay with me. Quite soon we met Eric and formed "Earthborn" and in due course Mike joined us as lead guitarist. This certainly wasn't my best or most enjoyable line up, especially as Eric's van always seemed to pick me up just as *Poldark*, my favourite TV programme, was starting! However, it was even more financially successful as we played either 2 or even, occasionally, 3 nights every week. If we ever were short of a gig I would make a telephone call to a busy agent, Bob Kember of Watford, who always came up with a gig, even if it was just for a drummer! As a result this became an important extra income for us.

One of the venues we played every couple of months or so was 'The Duck' at Aylesbury which just happened to be the 'local' for several of the staff from Stoke Mandeville Hospital where, at that time, Jimmy Saville was a real hero because of the huge amounts of money he was raising for the upgrading and rebuilding of parts of the hospital. One of the nurses who was a particular fan of ours said several times that she'd told Jimmy Saville about us and he said he'd come and see us and get us on TV! Unsurprisingly he never did.

One lasting memory of Earthborn was, following Dennis's emigration to Australia and finding ourselves short of a bass player, we invited Mike's friend Roger Newell to stand in with us in between his "day (evening??) job" with Rick Wakeman. Some 20 or so years later, Roger joined Marty Wilde's Wildcats and it was thanks to him that I was able to interview Marty for my YouTube channel in 2017. And I still have the first record I ever bought, way back in 1959, "Bad Boy" (written and recorded by, yes you've guessed it, Marty Wilde!) despite it never having recovered from being played at "slow speed" on my parents "wind up" gramophone!

This was also the time when package holidays to Spain had started. We would get requests for *Viva Espana* or *Spanish Eyes* from the audience. And, who drew the short straw as vocalist? Me! Fortunately the audiences weren't too demanding then or as one club manager put it: "After they've had a couple of drinks, all you need is a couple of monkeys and a dustbin"! Not true of course, but not so far off, all the same!

In the heady days of the '70s before the Internet, Social Media and Netflix etc., the clubs were always packed and the performers were the stars. Coupled with a job dealing with hairdressers, temptation was all around and sometimes irresistible.

Following the demise of Earthborn, Tony Price was probably the best vocalist and front man I ever worked with, and the person with whom I've most enjoyed performing. We played as a duo, trio or four piece or whatever the venue or our agents required, sometimes as Earthborn as I kept the name. We remained friends for the rest of his life. We even did a few gigs in Cornwall in the mid-80s after I'd moved there and when he came to stay. With the right promotion and a slice of luck Tony would have been the star he always deserved to be. His singing of the Marty Robbins classic *Devil Woman* and various Roy Orbison numbers was simply outstanding and almost always "brought the house down"!

Shortly after I was promoted at Clynol, the new Marketing manager, Tony Lunch decided to give me the task of organising the Clynol Cup which was the showcase for hairdressers to demonstrate their professional skills. In previous years Clynol's version of this competition had been a very poor imitation of that

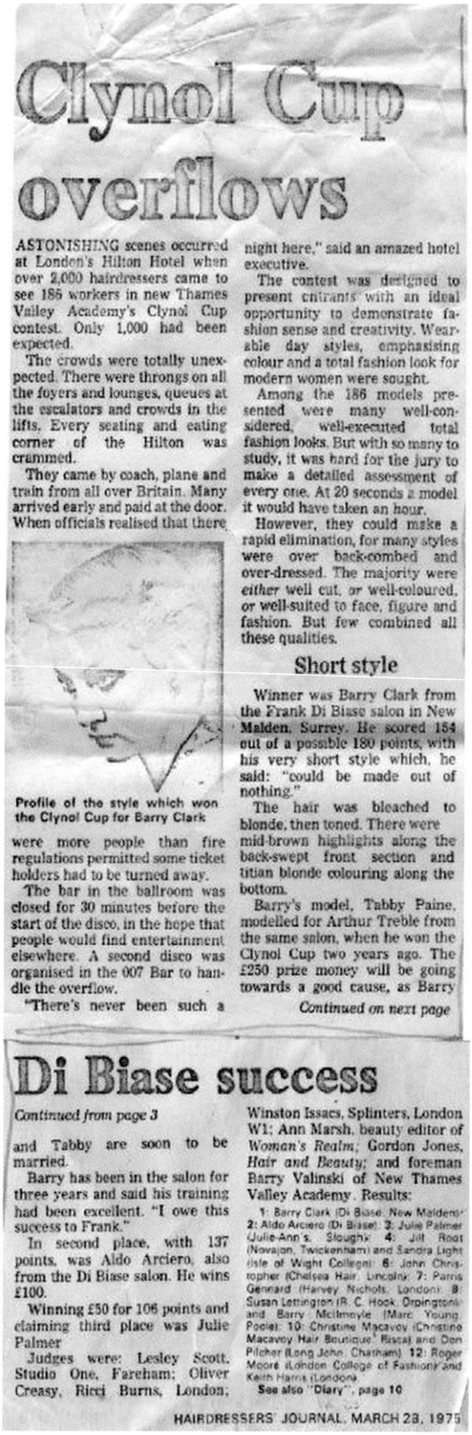

Clynol Cup overflows

ASTONISHING scenes occurred at London's Hilton Hotel when over 2,000 hairdressers came to see 186 workers in new Thames Valley Academy's Clynol Cup contest. Only 1,000 had been expected.

The crowds were totally unexpected. There were throngs on all the foyers and lounges, queues at the escalators and crowds in the lifts. Every seating and eating corner of the Hilton was crammed.

They came by coach, plane and train from all over Britain. Many arrived early and paid at the door. When officials realised that there,

Profile of the style which won the Clynol Cup for Barry Clark

were more people than fire regulations permitted some ticket holders had to be turned away.

The bar in the ballroom was closed for 30 minutes before the start of the disco, in the hope that people would find entertainment elsewhere. A second disco was organised in the 007 Bar to handle the overflow.

"There's never been such a night here," said an amazed hotel executive.

The contest was designed to present entrants with an ideal opportunity to demonstrate fashion sense and creativity. Wearable day styles, emphasising colour and a total fashion look for modern women were sought.

Among the 186 models presented were many well-considered, well-executed total fashion looks. But with so many to study, it was hard for the jury to make a detailed assessment of every one. At 20 seconds a model it would have taken an hour.

However, they could make a rapid elimination, for many styles were over back-combed and over-dressed. The majority were either well cut, or well-coloured, or well-suited to face, figure and fashion. But few combined all these qualities.

Short style

Winner was Barry Clark from the Frank Di Biase salon in New Malden, Surrey. He scored 154 out of a possible 180 points, with his very short style which, he said: "could be made out of nothing."

The hair was bleached to blonde, then toned. There were mid-brown highlights along the back-swept front section and titian blonde colouring along the bottom.

Barry's model, Tabby Paine, modelled for Arthur Treble from the same salon, when he won the Clynol Cup two years ago. The £250 prize money will be going towards a good cause, as Barry

Continued on next page

Di Biase success

Continued from page 3

and Tabby are soon to be married.

Barry has been in the salon for three years and said his training had been excellent. "I owe this success to Frank."

In second place, with 137 points, was Aldo Arciero, also from the Di Biase salon. He wins £100.

Winning £50 for 106 points and claiming third place was Julie Palmer.

Judges were: Lesley Scott, Studio One, Fareham; Oliver Creasy, Ricci Burns, London; Winston Issacs, Splinters, London W1; Ann Marsh, beauty editor of Woman's Realm; Gordon Jones, Hair and Beauty; and foreman Barry Valinski of New Thames Valley Academy. Results:
1: Barry Clark (Di Biase, New Maldens) 2: Aldo Arciero (Di Biase); 3: Julie Palmer (Julie-Ann's, Slough); 4: Jill Root (Nowajon, Twickenham) and Sandra Light (Isle of Wight College); 6: John Christopher (Chelsea Hair, Lincoln); 7: Patrick Gennard (Harvey Nichols, London); 8: Susan Lettington (R. C. Hook, Orpington) and Barry McIlmoyle (Marc Young, Macavoy Hair Boutique, Biscal) and Don Pilcher (Long John, Chatham); 12: Roger Moore (London College of Fashion) and Keith Harris (London).

See also "Diary", page 10

HAIRDRESSERS' JOURNAL, MARCH 28, 1975

held by Wella and L'Oreal. So, we decided to hold the competition at a top Hotel in London's West End and book Noel Edmunds and the famous band, Marmalade, and hoping that, for once, we'd get a good attendance - rather than the rather depressing turnouts we'd had in the past. There was lots of discussion in the office involving the Company Directors and, even up till the day itself, we had no idea whether our expensive gamble would pay off. Several of our colleagues feared the worst and said so! But Tony and I kept telling ourselves and anyone who'd listen that it would be alright on the night! with our fingers firmly crossed!

On the night, when the doors opened, Tony and I were busy welcoming guests in the hall and there did seem to be a lot arriving! The first thing we knew that something had gone wrong – actually I mean "gone right" – was when the hotel manager came to us in a panic about half an hour later telling us that he'd had to close the doors as the venue was full! We simply couldn't believe it but when we looked downstairs, the hotel foyer was crowded with hairdressers trying to get in and some who had even bought tickets in advance were refused entry! Others, looking to make a grand entry halfway through, couldn't get in! It was chaos and the hotel had never seen anything like it and they had staff everywhere trying to hold back a tide of hairdressers clamouring to get in!

Tony and I had never imagined in our wildest dreams that the show could be a sell-out so safety attendance limits had never crossed our minds!

As a result there were some very

unhappy Clynol customers. The Directors spent months afterwards placating them! but suddenly people including the trade press were talking about Clynol and as Oscar Wilde is quoted as saying: "There is only one thing in the world worse than being talked about, and that is not being talked about"!

Clynol certainly was talked about for months afterwards!

Following the Clynol Cup, I was promoted to Product Manager and given responsibility for shampoos and setting lotions including the launch of "Fullness" which gave thin hair an appearance of more "body". Hardly surprising as the product contained slivers of clear plastic! but it was a successful launch!

Following this, in 1976, I was given control of the Ladies Wig Division. It was a poisoned chalice! The wig business was in sharp decline yet for some unknown reason Clynol purchased Ginchy wigs for sale to hairdressers, Deltress wigs for sale to department stores and the franchise for Christian Dior and Pierre Balmain wigs. In a light-hearted effort to create some interest in wigs, Tony Lunch and I put a band together to play at the Clynol Christmas party and we all wore Ginchy wigs! But the reality was that there was nothing that could be done to prevent the decline in wig sales and so we looked out for another product to prop up this sad state of affairs. What we found was ear piercing!

A trip to the States had discovered that this was fast becoming a fashion statement and the new way to do it was with a gun rather than a needle. We quickly found a supplier for the gun and the studs, signed a sole agreement for the UK and we were off. In department stores we were just beaten by Clairol but we were the very first in hairdressing salons. It was a fabulous success and within 12 months this was the biggest selling product in Clynol's history! Today, as we all know, piercing is bigger business than ever!

My reward, a few hundred pounds a year increase in salary which now reached the (not very) dizzy height of £5,000 per annum! Consequently, when I was approached in 1977 by one of our overseas customers in Europe, to start up his business in the UK at a salary of £8,000 pa plus commission and an "executive level" car. I accepted with alacrity especially as Clynol was then in the process of moving their head office up to Yorkshire which would have meant me moving there too! The reason for the move? Entirely financial, as the chance of buying the franchise for a revolutionary new hair roller called "Click Lok" was more than our Directors could resist. It was a great idea, but it never worked although we authorised several expensive attempts at modification! The reality was that it had

Clynol Cup Management team. From left: Robyn Hoskyns-Abrahall, Sales Director, Tony Lunch, Marketing Manager, Albert Smith, Managing Director, Ken Hylton-Smith, Chairman, Guy Mackenzie, Product Manager, Unknown Salesman. In front the three winning models with winner, Tabby Paine, centre!

cost the company dear and the offer of a financially assisted move, which basically got the Company out of a financial black hole, was irresistible!

I stayed with the European company, who marketed ladies wigs and men's hair products – including a new lightweight and inexpensive hairpiece – until I left for the USA in late summer 1979. Having set up a network of dealers throughout the UK, this was exactly what I would do later in the States.

Over that time, I made several good friends and contacts, including Keith Forshaw of the Trend Group who I last saw when he visited us in Cornwall just before the second Covid-19 lock-down in 2021!

Whenever I went to Europe for a meeting, the Managing Director would meet me at the airport and take me for a really top-class meal. However, I always had to stay in his house in his smallest guest room, sleeping in the most uncomfortable camp bed which, like the room, was also very small! After dinner and before going to his home, my function was to drive him round his local red-light district so he could choose a female companion for the next hour or so! I then parked nearby waiting for him to emerge and take him home, which seemed only a few minutes away! He was a gambler both in life and in business and, for all I know, still is!

Back in 1976 the change of house had also made a big difference to Amanda because, after waking up every night 5 or 6 times (maybe partly due to the heat in the original house during summer) she started sleeping much better and was, in fact going through the entire night! Also, she was growing up and one of my greatest pleasures and memories is taking her for walks – short and slow at first but getting longer and faster as time went on! She was the dearest little girl!

The cost of this house was the same as the selling price for the previous one and with a higher income, I increased my mortgage by £4,000. This partly to renovate a cottage which Paulene had bought in St Just, Cornwall several years previously. Then the work only cost £2,400 – how times have changed! The cottage would always provide her with an income as a holiday let investment but secondly the increase would also give me a little extra working capital (£1,600) to add to my savings so I could realise the dream I'd first had in 1971 to buy property for investment.

With the lowest price in High Wycombe then £7,995, Buckinghamshire was out of the question but Cornwall wasn't! so I headed down to Cornwall and bought my first investment property – a one bedroom terraced cottage in Albert Street, Camborne for £1,200! By chance the market in Cornwall was rising and I sold it a few months later for £1,900 which resulted in me buying two more. One at £950 in Redruth and the other in Bartles Row, Tuckingmill for £1,200. I then sold the Redruth one for £1,650 and bought another in Bartles Row for £1,800. The neighbours there wanted to rename it "Mackenzie Row" as I now owned half the street. It only had 4 properties! I bought and sold several more including one in a village called Skinners Bottom and, although I'd never want to live anywhere with a name like that, someone did as I sold it soon afterwards for twice what I'd paid for it!

I travelled the length and breadth of England with my job and always looked round estate agents wherever I happened to be. Although my focus was in Cornwall, I ended up buying a property in Northants and also a small dilapidated cottage in Factory Row, Harlesden, Norfolk, for just £1,500 and, having repaired the roof, sold it for £5,000. In 1978 I bought the cottages at Town Place, Treskillard (for just £750) which I still own and they form part of the property portfolio that Sally and I own today!

In December 1977 my darling youngest daughter, Iona, was born and I can really say, yes, I was there! She is now well on her way to becoming a top Executive in the world of TV with executive producing credits to her name of shows such as *I'm a Celebrity, Get Me Out of Here* and *Love Island!*

MG5
An adventurous style —
the hairdressing success
story of this year.
One of the
"Miss Ginchy" collection.
Available in
heat resistant colours
1B, 2, 4, 6, 8, 10, 12,
18/22, 22, 32, 130.

Miss Ginchy Wigs by Clynol

Chapter 12
Stateside Calling
1979 – 1981

FOR SEVERAL YEARS, my marriage to Paulene had been "on the rocks". This is now in the past and she has been happily with Mike for 40 years so I'll merely say that we were quite simply on different trajectories. I loved my daughter, Amanda, very much and still do and despite the unexpected arrival of my dear Iona in 1977, a trip to the New York Hairdressing Show in March 1979 helped convince me that my future lay in a separation from Paulene. Although and as my divorce papers will show, I would have happily taken full responsibility for Amanda and Iona, this simply wasn't an option that would have had legal backing back then.

For many years I'd harboured a desire to live in the United States. The USA seemed the land of opportunity far away from the political crises that had bedevilled the UK since the early 1970s. So, in September 1979, I said goodbye to the European company I'd worked for since 1977 and armed with letters of introduction to 2 different American companies, one in California the other in Florida, I left the UK – but desperately sad to be so far away from my girls.

I appeared to be the person the company in California, Crown Royale International was looking for. Someone to start up a new division to market ready-made hair replacements, associated products and a magic lotion which supposedly regrew hair! This would take me throughout the whole of the USA, establishing dealers in each state.

They took me on and I was immediately made Vice President although I preferred to be known as "International Sales Manager" at the, even then, not very generous salary of $600 per month + 10% commission on sales, but with a car supplied and air fares reimbursed. I put together a marketing package and following the company launch for invited guests I collected my car and set off on the 3000 mile journey back to Connecticut, where I was then living, with the aim of establishing dealerships en route.

All went well. In the main, the dealers were, with a couple of exceptions, pleasant and receptive but a bland bunch although one, "George" in Kansas, Missouri, was the exception. Understandably, some were more worried about their very high profit margins rather than the product itself or, for that matter, what it looked like! The custom-made hair replacement products which many currently sold, not only looked like builders' hard hats with hair stuck on top but, actually successfully served that purpose when one got attacked with a crowbar a few years previously! And, this was unofficially a part of the company's sales pitch!

However, George was a real character and my first sightings of him were in a series of huge posters all along the freeway into the city. I met him and his delightful wife and we had dinner together to discuss business. After dinner he invited me to come with him to his favourite gay sauna. His poor wife looked pleadingly at me, hoping I could talk him out of this excursion but, alas, no. I, of course refused his offer, it simply wasn't for me, but I couldn't stop him going! George was very obviously disappointed, but we still remained friends although very little business was concluded. And, what business was done wasn't paid for. This, I learned later was also the case with: the posters on the freeway, his bodyguard (complete with loaded handgun) and the stretch limo he used! I've always wondered how on earth he managed it! Luckily we were down only a few hundred dollars! Some must have been owed a lot more.

I'll never forget that first road trip. It was simply amazing!

Initially I was driving on the old Route 66 replacement road. I really did visit: San Bernadino, Barstow, Kingman, Flagstaff, New Mexico, Amarillo and Oklahoma City, livin' the dream of the *Route 66* song – *If you ever plan to motor west, Travel my way, take the highway that is best. Get your kicks on route sixty-six* – but... backwards! I loved it! And, on YouTube you can find the last recording of *Route 66* by the Guy Mackenzie Trio in 2016 which mentions all these places!

The whole trip took me nearly a month and I drove almost 6,500 miles in my "compact" 6 cylinder Chevrolet Citation not daring to exceed the blanket 55mph speed limit. After all there were State Police on the ground as well police in helicopters – "bears in the air"!

Some of my time on the road was very memorable, indeed.

Driving through the eastern desert of S. California, I recall seeing a naked man running parallel to the road, but some distance away, with no evidence of any habitation, or vehicle anywhere near! Not even a road junction! Very odd!

Trying to use a map in a new country while driving is not easy, even at 55mph! I especially remember the helpful and friendly truckers who, seeing a little car which looked a bit lost would call me up on their CB radios. Fortunately I had one too. "Breaker, breaker 19 the little Chevvy with the California plates, are you lost good buddy?". Then, after helping me on my way, would give a few friendly toots on their air horns as they thundered past me, their 16 wheels higher than the roof of my car!

Of course I just had to detour to Las Vegas. Even then, when one could drive through the whole strip in a matter of minutes, I simply hated it. It seemed to me to just be gambling, prostitution and some overpriced and flashy venues with expensive entertainment. Each to his (or her) own I suppose! And now it's a hundred times more so... get me out of there!

I also made a detour to the Grand Canyon arriving very late and in the dark. I couldn't immediately find a motel so I bedded down in a lay-by as near as I could to where I thought I'd see it. When I woke up, I simply couldn't believe my eyes! I was right on the edge and the sun was rising over this 1 mile deep chasm. The colours were staggering! What an amazing sight and one I'll never forget!

One of my later sales trips saw me in Omaha, Nebraska with the temperature -20 degrees Fahrenheit below. My motel room had ice creeping round the door frame and the temperature inside just reaching 60F... and I had a plane to catch which had been delayed due to snow and ice! I couldn't help remembering Buddy Holly, The Big Bopper & Richie Valens leaving Des Moines, Nebraska some years previously in similar conditions, never to return alive.

Life on the road can be quite lonely and not ideal for a personal relationship especially in such a huge and diverse country as the USA. So once one has concluded the business meeting, books into a motel and has eaten "surf n turf" or some such delicacy, what to do? Watch boring TV? Unless the *ShanNaNa* show was on which I loved and still watch on YouTube, the next best thing is to find a bar and if that bar happened to be a "singles bar" so much the better! Just a few memories from those days and, if you are of a delicate disposition, skip the next few paragraphs. In Fresno, Ca. I went into the nearest bar and walked up to order a drink. There was a group of about 5 girls obviously on a night out, and one said to me something like: "I've been waiting for you all evening to take me home".

So, playing along with this, my reply was in the similar vein: "Really sorry I'm late, are you ready to go now?" To which she replied: "Yes, let's go" adding "are you for real?" To which I replied: "Yes, for sure but I just have to pay for my drink." Which I did but, I didn't have time to drink it! As we walked out to her nearby apartment, I could see her friends looking on in stunned amazement at their friend's "technique". Needless to say, a night of passion ensued which left me somewhat jaded for my business meeting the next day. Maybe these sort of experiences are commonplace today but they certainly weren't 40 years ago!

The bar I went into in Amarillo had an attractive female manager who said to me as I walked in: "Voulez vous coucher avec moi ce soir?". She was quoting a lyric from the song *Lady Marmalade* which was popular at that time! Translated the question is "Do you want to sleep with me tonight?"

My reply was: "Oui merci". So I chatted to her for the remainder of the evening until closing time and then we went back to her apartment which adjoined the bar. After a rather "exhausting" hour or so, I reached out to the table beside the bed for the glass of water that was left there but, in my semi-conscious state, only got hold of something cold with what felt like a handle at the end! It was a loaded handgun! I said why do you keep this beside your bed? Her cool reply was: "Well it's there in case someone breaks in and I always shoot first"! I spent a few nervous hours until I left as soon as I could.

I recall another bar in somewhere like Boston and it was dead! So I asked one of the male drinkers where the nearest good singles bar was. He said: "You're in luck, there is a bar which has a ladies' night tonight with male strippers." This was very unusual at that time. "When they leave and men are allowed in, they'll be fighting over you!" he added. So I joined a small throng of men waiting to be allowed in when the initial entertainment had finished.

As I walked in and looked round, a sea of faces looked in our direction but one blonde attractive woman on the other side of the room seemed to be signalling to me more than any other. Of course I wasn't certain if it was to me or not. But a few moments later she came over and said: "Didn't you see me waving at you?" I said that I did but wasn't sure it was me, but she replied: "Of course it was you."

We left soon after but she was reluctant to come to my motel room as, I might be a murderer – despite my "English accent!" and as she was married. Our initial venue that night was my car! So after some driving around, we managed to find a relatively quiet side street and parked up. Well, things were getting very "steamy" when a car drew up behind us with blue lights flashing. Within moments there was a banging on our car windows and powerful torches were shining in our faces or, more likely, the body parts on display! Of course it was the police and they wanted to know why we weren't in a motel room.

My companion was in a blinding panic in case her husband found out so in my best English Public School accent, truthfully, I said: "I'm awfully sorry officer, things just got out of hand". He asked me where I was from so I said "England" which was easier than explaining Scotland!

"Do you do this in your country?" he demanded. Of course I was full of apologies and said: "No". Then said, with a weary sigh: "I could have booked you, but I won't. Just don't let me catch you again". With his: "Have a good day" wishes ringing in our ears, we breathed a sigh of relief and after some discussion continued in my motel room, from where, a couple of hours or so later, she returned to hubby for, no doubt, a repeat performance!

Once, for a couple of days I found myself stuck in dreary downtown Louisville. Having got bored of the endless country music on the radio and TV channels full of preachers threatening fire and brimstone on the ungodly, I wandered into town and finding a rundown cinema showing XXX rated films, I paid my entrance fee and went in.

The films were as rundown as the cinema, which was almost empty. So I sat down in a quiet spot somewhere in the middle of the auditorium. Quite soon I became aware that a huge woman of Amazonian stature had come to sit beside me! I turned to look at her and was startled to see, in the gloom, that she had pulled up her skirt and was massaging what looked like her personal rain forest which had been underneath!

Her chat up line was: "Have you c**e?" I can't remember my reply but very soon I found out that she wasn't a "working girl" who I could have got rid of with something like… "sorry I've got no money darling" but an agency nurse who'd just come off her shift! So I made my excuses and left but, when I looked back, she looked well on her way to achieving with someone else what she hadn't managed with me! The doorman raised his eyes to me as I left but didn't offer me a refund!

Meanwhile, having set up a network of dealers for Crown Royale International throughout the USA and buoyed by this success, I decided to raise the matter of my meagre salary with my boss. He, obviously in a blind panic, immediately offered to double my salary to $1,200 per month and double my commission to 20% of all company sales! Obviously, and even to me, this was a ridiculously high offer but, never-the-less, I accepted!

However, some 8 months later he phoned me to say that I was making more than he or the company was and also that I was moving the company forward faster than they could cope with so would I take a reduction. My answer was an emphatic "No" and so buoyed with a "pay-off" I happily agreed to move on.

Frankly I'd had enough of the States, I'd been everywhere I'd wanted to go, seen everywhere I'd wanted to see including: the top of the World Trade Centre (the "Twin Towers"), the Empire State Building and been up the Statue of Liberty. I missed the way of life back in the UK but, most of all, I missed my daughters, who I loved very much.

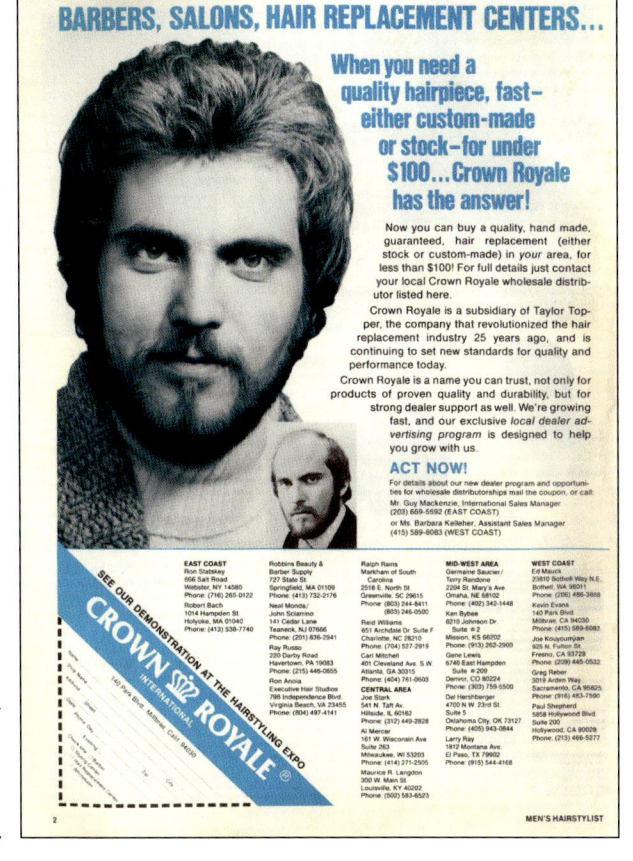

What my boss didn't know, was that my friend and past business associate, Keith Forshaw who owned the Trend Group of companies in Brighton, had already approached me to go into business with him marketing a range of small security products to the retail trade to help combat the crime wave that was fast becoming a major problem in the UK. The timing was just right and I accepted his offer and couldn't wait to return to the UK.

While in the States my financial war chest had been bolstered by several property deals. These included 3 building plots I bought in Florida on a bankrupt development site for just $2,850 which I sold for a profit, plus an "option" I'd bought on a piece of land, subsequently persuaded the local planning committee to grant planning permission on, and sold it later for substantial profit!

Before leaving this chapter of my life, I must mention two more involvements resulting from my time Stateside. One has now become a huge success in the UK but sadly not for me! Whilst the other which helped to kick-start a lifetime hobby which some might say has become my obsession.

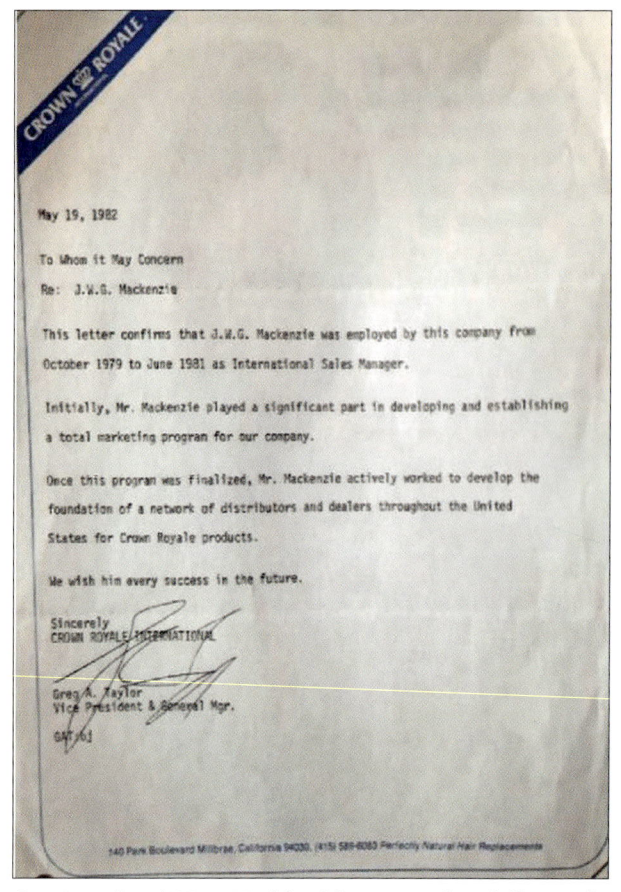

The first? Electric bikes! Something I'd never seen, or indeed, heard of in the UK. In early 1980 I saw an advert in a US national magazine, so I immediately headed down to New Jersey, where the company was based, to find out more. And having tried one and, despite finding out that the claimed "up to 25 miles on one charge" actually was nearer 12 miles, it did cost almost nothing to run and still seemed a "no-brainer" marketing opportunity for the UK. Full of enthusiasm, I negotiated temporary exclusivity for the UK and headed back to England via Freddy Laker's Skytrain budget airline as usual (just £59 London/ New York) with a complete bike under one arm and an add-on motor under the other!

On arrival in the UK, I immediately contacted various individuals and marketing organisations hoping (no, expecting!) that at least one would partner and more importantly! finance me in launching this new, inexpensive mode of transport! I was too far ahead of the times. Everyone I approached had the same or a similar reaction: "It will never sell here!".

However, the second involvement turned out to be my first step as an electric guitar collector! It happened this way. The Fender Coronado, a semi acoustic guitar, had been launched as a rival to Gibson's top selling 335. Alas, it proved not to be a success and lasted for only about 2 years in production but, for me even then, that was the attraction.

Over the years I'd bought and sold a few guitars – and other odds & ends too – for profit but none of them had "floated my boat". But, when someone I knew offered me his Coronado 11, dating from 1968, and in a genuine Fender matching case for just $150 (then just £75!), I couldn't refuse! I still have it today although the case is somewhat battered after several house moves but I think of it as the cornerstone of my collection of old, rare and unusual electric guitars, after all, it is the first guitar featured on my Website!

Ahead of his time – Guy on his electric bike a "No brainer" and a marketing opportunity that didn't take off back in 1981

Guy's Fender Coronado 11 purchased Stateside in 1971
began his life-long obsession collecting guitars

Chapter 13
Back in the UK – Starting Over
1981 – 1985

I RETURNED TO THE UK in the summer of 1981 and having accepted Keith Forshaw's offer to join him in his new security business, Trends Security Alarms Ltd (TSAS), based in Brighton with the option of a partnership, I decided to take a 2 month holiday. This would give me the opportunity to sort things out in England but, most important of all, spend time with my daughters, Amanda and Iona before I started work in September.

I needed somewhere to live. I had bought a 2 bedroom detached cottage in Syresham, Northants, in early 1979, for £10,500 on a 100% bank loan which I'd been unable to sell since. This was my obvious destination. The house was only part modernised (a glimpse of things to come!) but it did have all the basic facilities. So all I needed was a cooker, fridge, bed, chair, heater and TV then I could move in!

Not only about to begin a new career and with a house to modernise, I also joined a band – Equal Status. Why the name? well they had 2 female lead vocalists! Were we equal? Well, not really, as one of them didn't even own a microphone but borrowed mine when there wasn't another available! However, following a gig in Southend, some 2 hours away, for which we were paid in total £60 (£10 each!) I finally decided to hang up my drum sticks. With the advent of Disco music, it had finally become clear to me that I'd never make a living as a working musician so, from now on, decided to put my spare energies into property.

I also needed a car. Quite by chance it was a 10-year-old 2.8 manual Jaguar XJ6 in black with gold bumpers – hiding the rusty chrome! – that caught my eye and I snapped it up! So now I had a Cadillac in the States, which in due course I would ship back home, and a Jaguar in the UK! I was getting ahead of myself. On reflection the expression, "Fur coat and no knickers" comes to mind, not unknown trait for a Mackenzie even today!

Iona, Amanda and Guy with the black Jag

Then it was down to Cornwall and, with my girls, I visited every holiday destination possible including: Flambards at Helston and Paradise Park at Hayle. It was one of the happiest times of my life! Paulene, with the money from our divorce, had bought a modern detached bungalow with all the latest modern conveniences. It was situated in a small peaceful estate near St Day, not far from Redruth. She also had the holiday cottage in St Just which would help bolster her income and a smart black Renault Fuego sporty type car. There was also a new man in her life, Mike, who she is still with now over 40 years later! So I had a lot of financial catching up to do!

Amanda and Iona at Paradise Park, Hayle

In Cornwall I also found inexpensive bed and breakfast accommodation in a modernised and very comfortable cottage nearby. It was owned by a friendly young couple which served me very well in the early days whenever I visited. However, some months later, and after her husband had gone to work, I walked out of my room and almost into my landlady who was standing outside my door with a welcoming smile on her face but completely naked! I was tempted, yes, but the last thing I needed was an irate husband or to be involved in another divorce so, giving her an equally friendly smile, I politely declined what was on offer, paid my bill but never went back!

For the next few years, until I moved to Cornwall to set up my own business in 1986, I found very comfortable B & B accommodation at a large house in Clinton Road, Redruth owned by a delightful retired couple. They often spoke about the house next door, 1 Clinton Road, which was even larger. Originally built for a sea captain it was now owned by a major local landlord, a Mr Roberts, and rented off as 15 bedsits!

Interestingly, some years later I was elected as a councillor on Kerrier District Council where I got to know Glyn Roberts, who represented Portreath, and we became good friends. He and I, then as Chairman, served on the Board of Kerrier Direct Services which became the first in-house contractor in the Country to make enough profit to be able to hand back some of its surplus to its client, in this case, Kerrier District Council!

My friend Keith Forshaw had originally been involved in ladies hairdressing but, in his early 20s had cleverly foreseen the 1960's boom in ladies wigs and, as a consequence, had become a major player in the UK market netting himself a fortune! However, that was now far behind him and although he was a major supplier of men's hair replacements which had resulted in me first meeting him in the '70s, he had been looking for a main market opportunity ever since.

He had now sourced an impressive range of inexpensive security products including: door alarms, window alarms, personal alarms plus the remarkable Repulse spray. This was a small aerosol which, when used in self-defence, emitted a disgusting smell as well as covering the assailant with a red dye! Keith was in charge of marketing and finance while I was responsible for sales. However, after considering the partnership he had kindly offered me for about a year I passed on it and put what money I had into property.

We launched TSAS at a trade show, gained a lot of interest, and I set about making appointments throughout the UK to turn that interest into sales. Interestingly, nearly every business I saw, whether they were small hardware shops or multi nationals, all bought a range of the products because, quite simply, we were in the fore front of a fast-expanding market. However, due to the lack of national advertising (which we had no budget for) and a lack of point-of-sale displays meant that many outlets simply didn't reorder.

Our biggest customer was Argos and their initial order was for £15,000 and, as part of my income came from commission, this netted me £1,500.

Another substantial customer turned out to be Harrods of Knightsbridge and I always enjoyed seeing their friendly buyer in his minute office – a cupboard – behind his sales counter! Parking was a nightmare, even in those days, and I always ended up parking on a yellow line having left a suitable note which usually started: "Dear traffic warden…". Amazingly I never got a parking ticket!

One other customer who sticks in my mind was the large hardware shop I visited in Liverpool. I carefully parked in a side street, not on yellow lines this time! and went into the shop asking for the owner. When he saw me, he immediately asked: "Where have you parked?". I told him and he told me to park in front of the shop, to which I replied there are double yellow lines there! His response was that it's better to park there and risk a parking ticket rather than getting back to your car and finding the wheels gone or, more likely, the car! I did as he suggested and, unsurprisingly, in that part of the 'Pool' a substantial sale was achieved! Of course, every retailer who contacted us (especially in Liverpool) wanted the Repulse spray. However quite soon it was pointed out to us that it contravened the Firearms Act so, sadly, it had to be withdrawn! So, if there are any about now, who knows, they may just be collectable!

I got down to Cornwall at every opportunity to spend time with Amanda and Iona. In due course, a girlfriend I had for a short while, introduced Amanda to horses and it was love at first sight! Consequently, every day after school and every weekend Amanda was at her local riding stables helping out, taking rides out and occasionally riding too which resulted in her becoming an excellent and extremely hardworking horse woman. Occasionally she even got paid. £1!

By 1982, I'd found a buyer for Syresham. I made all of £500, but I had lived free! I then bought 99 Manor Road, Brackley, a terraced one up/one down cottage for £11,250. It had a welcoming atmosphere and I think of this cottage now as not only my first home back in the UK but also the start of the property business

Iona and Amanda with their rosettes

99 Manor Road

which I now own, with my wife Sally. The property was not modernised when I bought it so, once again, I lived in the bedroom and used the downstairs just for cooking! I managed to get a local authority grant to pay for much of the modernisation and I did the painting and finishing off in the evenings and at weekends.

All I needed now was an accountant to help sort my depleted and confused finances. The Estate Agents, who sold me 99 Manor Road, recommended me to a young accountant, David Upstone. David remained my accountant until his retirement in 2018 and "en route" extricated me from a couple of potential financial disasters during that time too! Since then Anita Brook has bought his practice and, ably assisted by her efficient team, have proved themselves every bit as good as David and a pleasure to deal with too!

Back in Cornwall, I'd managed to get the planning permission altered to allow the construction of two properties on the building plot which I'd be able to hang onto following my "Full and Final" divorce settlement and valued then at £2,000 which was a bonus. But, I was starting to despair of gaining planning consent, after three failed applications and an appeal dismissed, on my derelict properties at Town Place, Treskillard which were valued at just £1,000 in my divorce. Then, out of the blue, the agents who had acted on my appeal told me of a letter and telephone call they'd received, from a Mr. Bill Shenton who was highly respected locally but had chosen the life of a tramp, apparently after his wife had left him! He asked for £10 for his advice as to how I could get round the planning consent issue for Treskillard! I still have his beautifully written letter. Basically his advice, when I met him, was just move into the property, do it up as you go and ignore the Planning Department! I then discussed his suggestions with my architect.

This was, in effect, what we did and got another local authority grant in the process! The result was that, just one year later, I had my first tenant! And, long

Town Place, Treskillard before and…

Town Place, Treskillard after

story short, soon ended up with another property there which I also rented out! Every year these two properties gross more income than their total cost and I still own them today. How did Bill Shenton know about me and why did he decide to try and help me? I'll never know, but I have always considered it… Karma.

Eventually I sold No.99 in 1984 for £19,000 and bought Treen Cottages at Gurnards Head near Zennor, for just £20,000 with a mortgage of £18,000. This was a terrace of 5 un-modernised cottages. I'd now decided that, sooner or later, I was going to make my home in Cornwall which was a county that I loved since my first visits in the 1970s. Here I'd be nearer to my daughters too.

However, just before I committed myself to the purchase, Elwyn Thomas of the selling agents, Lodge & Thomas, very honourably rang me with a caution. He warned me that there would be a real issue with the farmer who owned the farm behind as he was claiming a right of way through the access to the property - for his cows! Not only that, but he hoped that by frightening off any prospective purchasers, he would be able to buy for his top offer of £2,000!

What? Me worry! I told him that I was up for the challenge. Little did I imagine then the bitter dispute which was to come. It ended up in Court in 1987 but, thankfully, the Judge's decision was in my favour! And remarkably, not long afterwards, we all ended up friends. Not close, perhaps, but on good terms anyway as we still are, although the farmer has long since passed away! The best house in that terrace is still part of my property portfolio and the current tenants have now clocked up 30 years there!

In late 1984 Keith rang to tell me that he'd agreed to sell TSAS to Polycell. He asked me if I'd be prepared to be part of the package to help them launch this range of products which was completely new to them. I was entirely happy to go along with this as, in any case, I hoped to make my life with my own property business in Cornwall in the near future. The offer they made me included an almost overgenerous expenses package! Polycell were a strange bunch with a top-heavy Sales Management team, having just made a number of salespeople redundant but, at the same time, increasing the sales targets of the remainder! Some of the Sales team who were in my grade, were suspicious of me not only because I was an incomer but also the company car which came with me was a Ford Sierra GL automatic whereas my grade in Polycell only merited a vehicle

Treen Cottages as they were when Guy moved in 1986

Reunited: Tony (Price) & Guy playing live in Penzance 1987 when Tony and his wife would visit Guy at his Treen cottage

with a manual gearbox and an L designation! It didn't matter to me as I only saw this as a temporary job. Apart from anything else, I'm not a big company person. However, I did have a day or two at the races with them and a stay in the Gleneagles hotel!

Meanwhile, having sold 99 Manor Road and with one cottage at Treen still having minor works to make it habitable for me, I needed somewhere to live. So I contacted Martin Kennedy-Bell. Martin had just come through a divorce but had managed to hold onto his huge detached house in Chiswick, London which he still owns! He immediately agreed to rent me a room and I had 15 enjoyable months there!

Martin's extraordinary hobby was driving coaches, something I still don't understand. This seemed to involve him with every "singles" organisation in London! He knew all the best venues for a couple of single men of uncertain age!

Our favourite was the aptly named Winning Post Hotel near Twickenham! One girl who I met there was a slim, vivacious blonde who only drew breath from talking to smoke a seemingly endless supply of cigarettes! But she was lovely and having ended up in her bed and following, for me, a relaxing romantic encounter with her, despite the cigarettes and chatter, realised that she hadn't experienced the same satisfaction as me!

However, after a short time she had obviously worked out that I was unable to do for her what she'd done for me, she said, do you mind if I do this. "This" happened to be the biggest pile of Men's magazines I'd ever seen (making me look a beginner), hidden under her bed! I said that's fine with me (being as broad minded as anyone at that time) assuming that the pictures of the ladies were in this case, the attraction for this lady! But not so, every magazine seemed to be "dogeared" or folded on pages with writing so it was the X-rated stories which floated this particular boat – not, in fact, the ladies displaying all! So and without going into unnecessary detail, I'll just say that, after an interlude with her reading material and me as a spectator, this lady was purring peacefully beside me but, thankfully, the smoking and talking had ended – for a while anyway!

All good things do come to an end. Polycell offered me the hoped for redundancy package, which I immediately accepted. Then I thanked Martin for his hospitality and on 2nd February 1986 I set off for my new life as a residential landlord and property developer in Cornwall. My new home being, once again, a partly modernised one up/one down cottage at the far end of Treen Cottages (which I named Treen End Cottage) but I had just about enough money, including more grants, to renovate all the cottages, prior to renting the other four out. So this chapter of my life finished, as it had begun, with me living in a semi-modernised cottage accompanied by my cooker, fridge, bed, chair, heater, and TV as my constant companions!

Farmer T's indomitable troops

Chapter 14
War in the West (Cornwall that is!)
1986 – 1987

THE TRACK off the St Ives to St Just road led past the Gurnards Head Hotel to the coast. On the left-hand side just before my properties, Treen Cottages, was Treen Farm owned by Farmer T. and on the right-hand side and almost opposite my properties was also Treen Farm but, this one was owned by Farmer B. The land on the left-hand side was owned by Farmer T. and the land on the right-hand side was owned by Farmer B. Their milking parlours were almost opposite each other and on opposite sides of the track. However, the only way that Farmer T. could get his cows into his milking parlour without driving them past his front door was via my land which also provided the only access to my properties! Both farmers were of similar age and had owned their farms for a similar time but each vied to be top dog! Farmer T. had 3 sons of similar ages to Farmer B.'s 3 daughters. Seemingly every day when milking time arrived, both sets of cows would be brought in at about the same time and, the herds would get muddled up and this was always followed by shouting and swearing and this had been a way of life for as long as anyone could remember!

Farmer B. was a lovely man but he did have a quick temper, evidenced by the battle scars his tractor displayed from the days when it wouldn't start, but I always got on well with him and also with his delightful wife who was more "Hampstead" (her family came from that area of London) than Gurnards Head. But his opening gambit to me was, what are you going to do with these properties? I replied that I was going to renovate them and rent them out as permanent homes. I remember his reply well: "Who the hell do you think is going to want to rent a property down here?!" I could see his point as this area was then far removed from the gentrified location it is now!

This area of West Cornwall had, in 1971, been the setting and location for Sam Peckinpah's psychological thriller *Straw Dogs*. The film starred Dustin Hoffman and Susan George. The plot involves an 'incomer' played by Hoffman who buys a property near to his Cornish wife's former village home. He's looking for some peace and quiet to finish a book he is writing. Suffice to say he is not welcomed by the locals, some of whom he employs to renovate the property. Returning to her Cornish roots, his wife (Susan George) has 'history' which allows the situation to escalate into full blown terror, a horrific rape and bloody violence as the locals lay siege to the property. Controversial at the time, *Straw Dogs* is now regarded as one of Peckinpah's best films. Quite possibly because the conflict between incomers and the locals is an all too familiar situation which lends credibility to the film. In various degrees of severity this situation probably happens everywhere but it is particularly true of Cornwall which hangs on dearly to its Celtic heritage. As a Scot I can understand this and by contrast Cornwall has a fine reputation for hospitality. These conflicts often result in a good argy bargy, lot of swearing, stress and sometimes court cases, but in my experience never violence.

However, I was now in "Straw Dogs" country for sure! I especially realised this when Farmer T's opening gambit to me was: "You don't own nothing down here, I own all this land" – pointing to the access to my properties which he was driving his cows through as he spoke! I politely pointed out that I'd bought the land with the properties. Whereupon, he said and I also remember this well: "I'm going to drive you back to where you came" and also: "You're a foreigner"! I replied that maybe I was but my architect wasn't as he came from Penzance! To which he replied: "He's a foreigner too"! Gradually I got to know the few others who lived nearby and I became aware that Farmer T. really was a "village Hampden... the little tyrant of his fields..." as he'd managed to stop one of the houses further down the track getting mains electricity and, the one at the end, having mains electricity and telephone – by the sheer power of his personality! I started to realise that I hadn't just moved west but rather that I'd moved to the "wild west" which it really was then! Later on I discovered that Farmer T. had laid a drainage pipe to drain the effluent from his milking parlour, through my land and under the track which,

Farmer T's troops – on the march!

almost unbelievably, discharged outside Farmer B's back door! Amazingly the pipe had been in situ' for several years and, although a lot of swearing and shouting occurred, nothing had been done about it.

Despite all this, I remained positive and felt sure that one way or another, I'd somehow win through. Consequently, I started work on the 3rd and 4th cottages as the first two were basically habitable, despite having to wade ankle deep though cow slurry! I did have some building contacts in Penzance and ended up with an occasional (subject to any of them not being called away by their main employer... the job centre!) team of semi-skilled, slightly skilled and entirely unskilled labour. Well they were cheap, £15 a day was top whack! The plumbing and electrics were undertaken by tradesmen who worked for cash, of course! As did my excellent plasterer who, on £20 a day, had to be paid daily as he always had an evening appointment with his favourite pub! They were, in the main, a cheerful bunch who made light of the daily visits of the cows and kept telling me I'd win through in the end!

We even had a couple of costly (for me!) nights out in Penzance when my musical friend, Tony Price came to stay for a week each year with his wife. Once again as Tony & Guy, we did a couple of gigs locally and everyone working for me was invited!

My own role, apart from chief bottle washer (that's a joke, by the way!), was

The slurry left in the access

foreman, and building supplies gopher! For those I had to travel to the far side of Penzance to the then biggest supplier, UBM Pratts! Not only were they aptly named and hugely overstaffed but whenever I turned up they all seemed to be either just off on: morning crib break, a lunch break or afternoon tea time! Was it my imagination or did the yard staff really enjoy watching my frustration as they swilled down yet another cup of tea, chattering to each other as they did so? I still wonder what happened to them all when the Company went out of business a few years later.

On one occasion, during the midst of my later legal battle with Farmer T., I had over loaded my car's roof rack with plasterboard sheets, I stopped suddenly at a pedestrian crossing in Penzance, whereupon all the sheets shot off into the road – luckily no one was harmed! As I was trying to put them back, who should stop and help, none other than Farmer T.'s solicitor who just happened to be walking past! Would that have happened in London? I think not!

As the properties began to take shape and the option of renting them became nearer, there had to a showdown with Farmer T. As a starting point I offered him a deal, let's split the land behind so you have an access for your cows and I have an access for my houses and, as sweetener, I said I'd pay him £2,000 compensation. This actually seemed to make him more angry and he then threatened to knock my houses down with his "tractor".

Farmer T. blocks my access with his tractor and muck spreader

This actually was an old JCB and, at that time, he was one of the few farmers in Cornwall who owned one. Consequently, I had no option but to take him on so I got in touch with a young solicitor in Penzance who advised me to block the access track! I, therefore, ordered 20 tons of hardcore which was then dumped on my land blocking the route to his milking parlour. When the cows tried to get though as they usually did, they couldn't and that was when all hell broke loose!

Farmer T. drove onto my land with his "tractor" and started to clear the way for his troops, his cows! in the front line to reach their home for the night, ably abetted by his 3 sons, while a few spectators stood by and watched the fun! Fun, it wasn't for me anyway and I called the police who at least ensured that I survived to tell this tale! The following week my young solicitor applied for a temporary injunction to stop Farmer T. trespassing on my land which was duly granted! However, this all depended on the full hearing which was to come in due course.

When the case eventually came to Court in 1987. I'd already promised Farmer B. that if I won, I'd get the drain removed. Strangely enough it was all quite amicable as Farmer T. backed down prior to the hearing and, in due course, I had the offending drain removed as promised! That night we celebrated and I still regret not buying a second bottle of whisky as the only bottle was quickly demolished by Farmer B.

Farmer T. clearing the hardcore Guy had blocked the access with

From then on, life at Gurnards Head would never be the same again and, in a short space of time, electricity and telephone were connected to the 2 properties which had waited so long for them!

Strangely, almost from that moment on, Farmer T's sons became quite friendly with me and they never bore me a grudge merely saying: "Father's a hard man"! I even visited a couple of local nightclubs with one! Today if I visit Gurnards Head and I see any of them, I either get a friendly toot from a tractor or hear a voice behind me saying: "All right Guy boy"! Just as oddly though, Farmer B's daughters never really took to me! Was it because of my "open door policy" for female visitors which didn't include any of them? But, for the record, I'd just say that I was always very much aware of their father's short temper and his poor battered tractor.

One night during this somewhat stressful period of my life, I visited the cinema in Penzance and saw a film I then knew nothing about, *Straw Dogs*! A few disturbed nights followed, not so much because of the 'horror' but because of the actor who played the part of the chief agitator among the locals, Peter Vaughan, who did a brilliant job. Coincidentally, he bore a striking resemblance to Farmer T.

I had enjoyed most of my time at Gurnards Head but now it was time to move on. I had sold the first two cottages which had covered all my costs including the mortgage. Looking through the local paper, I saw that a smallholding with several acres of land and far reaching sea views was for sale near Helston. I looked at it on the day it was advertised without being able to even get inside and even knowing it was only served by a cold tap plus a "bucket and chuck it" outside, I agreed to purchase it. I moved in in 1989 and it has been my home ever since. In case you are wondering, those "facilities" have now been completely updated!

Treen Cottages completed

Chapter 15
Just for the Record: Herland Barns, Godolphin – 1988

1988 DAWNED with me living in Treen Cottage, the last of the properties I'd renovated at Treen and, as a bonus, this one was habitable and complete! So now, with time on my hands, I looked out for another development opportunity and the best I could find was a beautifully constructed range of stone barns at Herland Farm, Godolphin. The barns may have been right but the price wasn't at £90,000 and with planning consent for only 3 dwellings and workshops. Without any expectation of having my offer accepted, I tabled £60,000. Evidently the vendor was keen to sell and having agreed to include an adjoining field in the deal, we settled on a price of £62,500!

It now occurred to me the best way forward was in partnership with a builder. Paulene's partner Mike (Bingo) and his dynamic workmate, Derek, had undertaken completing the major part of Treen Cottage which included reworking the engineer's drawings so the cross beams upstairs didn't mean ducking every time one walked in that part of the cottage. Their work had been excellent so I decided to offer them the opportunity to join me. Unfortunately, by now Mike had fallen out with Derek so it was Bingo or nothing and, as a result, I chose him as partner and site foreman but, just in case, I remained in overall control.

Initially building works went well and the economy seemed to be with us too, due to a sudden rise in property prices. We'd estimated that each barn would cost in the region of £20,000 to convert, not including bank interest on a 100% loan, and Barn No.1 had a sales estimate of £65,000 in April 1988! No fortune even then, but a profit nevertheless!

However, within a short timescale, the resale estimate was in the region of £85,000 so things were looking even better than anticipated!

However, clouds were on the horizon! A couple of months into the job, Bingo arrived on site with

Barn no 1 and the single storey extension which was slated and then had to be stripped and re-slated!

a skinny young lad in tow saying this is "mah boy" who wants a job. Under the circumstances, I agreed, but at the Gurnards Head rate for "not very skilled/ totally unskilled" labour of £2/hr. From day one, he was at odds with the other workforce. They objected to his "know all" attitude (as I did) and kept telling me tales about him. These I ignored, until it transpired that he'd slated the entire single storey roof to Barn No. 1 extension with natural slates laid on batten but with just one nail at the top of the slate (rather than two about a third of the way down). Quite honestly it looked good until one realised that a sudden wind could completely strip the roof! Bingo was foreman! so I hadn't noticed until it was pointed out to me. This really was a major "cock up"! The roof would now have to be stripped and re-slated correctly resulting in a huge extra and unnecessary cost!

Although Bingo was the foreman he was absent at the time. I decided to sack "mah boy" immediately after he'd told me he'd slated the roof with one nail because it was quicker! I then, symbolically, took his shovel off him as he appeared then to be digging up the foundations of the extension and he didn't seem to know why! I didn't either! As casual labour paid in cash, giving him notice wasn't an issue.

However, being only a young lad, his lip quivered and tears filled his eyes which made me feel that I'd been somewhat harsh so I said I'd discuss it with Bingo when he returned. Consequently, I agreed "mah boy" could work out a couple or so weeks' notice because, as Bingo unsurprisingly whined: "He's got nothing else". For the remainder of his time at Herland, I put "mah boy" on "needle gun" duties i.e. cleaning off exposed stonework.

There was now an unpleasant atmosphere on the site. Bingo's frequent absences from Herland were occasioned by an over reliance on his memory. He wouldn't make lists of the materials we needed on his trips to the builders merchant and kept arriving back on site having forgotten something! This had been something of an irritation and following the disaster of "mah boy's" roofing misadventure I realised that I could run the job better on my own. Consequently, I made Bingo an offer to buy him out. My young solicitor told me it was far too generous, but I wanted him gone and anyway I knew that the offer was one that Bingo wouldn't and couldn't refuse! He didn't refuse, signed the initial documentation immediately and drove off! Today on the very rare occasions I run into Bingo, we enjoy a friendly talk about vintage British motor cycles… but steer clear of building!

In November 1988, Barn No. 1 was sold at the top of the market for a whopping (then) £112,500! My decision to extract Bingo, despite my solicitor's misgivings, had proved correct. I sold another barn unconverted, built and sold 6 starter homes on the field that came with the original purchase. I still retain a separate single storey barn originally designated as a workshop which I converted to residential accommodation and have rented for exactly 30 years. And now, over 30 years later, I've been able to recently remind my not-so-young solicitor that I did get it right at the time, after all!

Chapter 16
The End of the Beginning
1989

LOOKING BACK, I really think of 1989 as the end of the beginning, as it was the year I met Sally who has been such an important part of my life ever since.

Having sold Barn No. 1 at Herland Farm and made some money in the process, I now had time to think about what to do with the remaining barns and, in the meantime complete some "finishing off" in my new home. It had been "modernised" in a way I'd not experienced in the homes I'd owned during the previous 8 years, apart from the kitchen as I'd run out of money by then! This just had two old base units and a sink plus a piece of mature worktop balanced between boxes! The outside had to become less of a builders' yard and dumping ground. Fortunately, I had Malcolm helping me who was almost my first tenant at Treskillard, had been with me all through Treen and, for that matter, Herland as well. Malcolm sadly died a few years ago so now I feel that it's safe to reveal he was on the dole, supported by housing benefit and so, in his/our situation, cash was king, even if it was only a small amount!

I had also bought the field next to Treskillard and, for a time until the Council served an enforcement notice, had a couple of residential caravans sited there and rented out. As the main sewer and water ran through the field, this made the whole process very easy and inexpensive for the tenants as we never made the relevant authorities aware of these connections!

However, in June, my life was about to change forever when I met Sally – a beautiful, tall, slim elegant blonde girl, 6 years younger than me who is also brave,

Sally in 1989, off to the beach

determined and with an almost unrivalled work ethic. She was the one who wasn't going to get away. I immediately reversed my "open door policy" dating back to Gurnards Head and we've been together ever since and married for almost 25 years! Sally has been at my side ever since then, not least, when cleaning properties in the rental portfolio we subsequently built up together over the years (some were, to say the least, unhygienic!) so we always had a lightning quick turnaround and at minimal cost too!

When Sally moved in with me a few weeks after we met it wasn't just her! She came with her two Newfoundland show dogs, Rosie and Bunty (Sally has been successfully showing pugs for the last 10 years), her German shepherd cross, Wolfy (he did look like wolf to me!), Chloe, a Pekingese and two cats, Bella (a large black cat who liked to sit on my lap when I watched cricket on TV) and a dear little Devon Rex called Nancy who used to sit on my shoulder. Very sadly, before the year was out, Nancy had died after a brave battle with leukaemia.

But for my birthday, Sally bought me a Rottweiler dog who I called Bruno. He had a wonderful temperament and everyone who visited our house had to be introduced to him as I was so proud of him. I loved taking him for walks, he was the most handsome and friendliest dog imaginable and I was heartbroken when he died barely 9 years later.

Somehow the sun always seemed to shine in the summer of 1989 and Sally and I visited nearly every beach in West Cornwall. And we also had some wonderful times with Amanda and Iona, including a memorable visit to Tintagel (which I'd never been to) and a couple of visits to the Chinese restaurant in Camborne which was then the height of local fine cuisine! But I also used to see my girls on my own, as I'd used to, before I met Sally.

Iona with Sally, 1989

In early autumn, my sister Lucy invited us all to visit her in her home near Rome. Having been used to doing everything as economically as possible, I booked the budget airline to beat all budget airlines. I don't like flying at the best of times so the flight over was nerve wracking in the extreme (!), not least for poor Iona. Luckily she sat next to a priest who kept her, and us all, as calm as possible!

In those far off days before Maastricht, we had

to produce our passports at Rome airport. So on arrival, we queued up and waited patiently for our turn to go through the barrier for immigration. However, on the other side of the barrier, we suddenly noticed Lucy's husband Georgiou waving at us, telling us not to wait and just to come through a side gate ignoring the customs officials – his company supplied the fuel for the airport! This is what we did, feeling like VIPs in the process! He then drove us back to their beautiful home on the outskirts of Rome.

Not only was Georgiou a delightful, old fashioned gentleman and a perfect host throughout our stay, as was Lucy, but we'd also been bought gifts which were given to us on arrival. Mine was a beautiful leather briefcase of a quality I'd never even seen before, or for that matter, since; it had been several years since I'd visited Harrods and then not as a customer! Lucy had several cats, most of them she'd rescued, and Georgiou did mention to us once or twice, that he "lived in a zoo"! which, of course, It wasn't!

Over the week or so that we were there, we visited several Roman remains and even went in the Catacombs, an extraordinary experience! Amanda and Iona also had the opportunity to ride some of the horses they owned and to get to know their daughter, Vittoria, who is now an internationally acclaimed event rider but was only six then.

Georgiou also generously (and courageously!) let me take Amanda, Iona and Sally out on Rome's notorious roads in his Bentley! A driving treat for me but completely nerve wracking as cars cut us up, overtaking us on both sides, all the while waving at us and me driving three blonde girls around in an expensive car! Somehow I got back safely with the car and its passengers intact but, to this day, I'm not sure how!

After a fabulous holiday, it was time to brave that budget airline back to the UK! And, brave it we had to as it was tossed around in a storm and even had to make an unscheduled pit stop for more fuel on the way home. We never found out why? We eventually arrived safely although somewhat green around the gills –

Amanda at Flambards

with me saying, never again. I seldom flew after this and then only when absolutely necessary!

By now I'd already met Sally's mother and we'd got on extremely well but, the next step was for Sally to meet my mother. Hearing good reports from Lucy, she decided to come and stay with us for a few days. After a short time getting to know each other, Sally and my mother became firm friends and, in fact, she and her cat, Taurus lived with us for four of the last seven years of her life. When my mother died in 2002 her last words were to Sally, while holding her hand, "I love you" and she did. Sally's mother also lived with us for her last two years and we still miss both of them very much.

I'll end this chapter as I began. The year 1989 really was the end of the beginning for me. With Sally's help, some luck plus good Karma, lots of good things were still to come! Some sad times, some good times, a few bad and occasionally ugly ones too.

By the eve of my 25th Wedding Anniversary on the 28th February 2021 I can say that I had achieved nearly everything I'd ever hoped to achieve and a lot more that had never ever occurred to me, all those years ago.

Iona and Amanda with cousin Pam and her dogs in the late 1980s

Author's note: My cousin Pam (Pamela) Forbes was the daughter of my Great Uncle Col. Ronald Forbes and his first wife, the renowned explorer, travel writer and novelist of the 1920s and '30s, Rosita Forbes. Pam advised and supported me from the time my mother was first seriously ill in 1985/6 and for the rest of her life. I'll never forget the help she gave me

Chapter 17
The Big Bangs of 1990 aka "The Man with his Stone!" 1989 – 1990

THE BIG BANGS occurred at the end of 1989 but the repercussions continued well into 1990. The year of 1989 had been a turning point in my life. Thankfully, Sally had got on well with Amanda and Iona and the year had up to now been both magical and memorable but was, at the very end, about to become unforgettable – for all the wrong reasons!

Nancy, Sally's little cat sadly died aged only three which upset us both for a long time. We also had the problem of what my mother referred to as "The Man with his Stone!" and this is how that all came about.

In those days I was still relatively new to renting out properties. I probably didn't check out prospective tenants in the way I do now and this was a big mistake! For reasons that will become obvious I'll call this tenant "Sylvest" who approached me asking to rent one of my houses. He offered to pay two month's

Iona, Sally and Amanda in 1996

rent as deposit and a month's rent in advance because he had no references. Somehow, I had a bad feeling about him right from the start. He stood 6'6" and weighed 245 lbs (over 111kg) and had something of a reputation. Yet – I still took him on, whilst reassuring myself that with the cash in hand everything would work out.

All went relatively well for a few months until Sylvest decided he wanted to buy a house for himself but, with only a small deposit and, on paper, a modest income, he was unable to proceed. He had found his perfect house and negotiated a good price but wanted me to come in with a 50/50 share. Initially, I agreed as he assured me he could come up with a substantial down payment for his share then rent my half at a figure that did, on paper, stack up. The purchase moved ahead but, just prior to exchange, Sylvest informed me that he didn't in fact have any deposit and asked me to go ahead on a 50/50 ownership basis and he would pay his share, part rent and part mortgage, to me.

Without his financial commitment, I decided that this was a step too far for me so I refused his proposal but bought the property myself thinking, as it turned out correctly, that I could resell it at a profit. Of course, and having had his first property purchase, as he saw it, snatched away at the 11th hour, Sylvest was not a happy bunny – even though I offered to split any profit on a resale with him. Did I say bunny? He certainly didn't turn out to be a bunny, more a raging elephant!

Of course, the difficult part of all this "a wheelin' n' a dealin' " was that he was still my tenant! Late-night phone calls began with associated threats. These involved fire (my house) and blood (mine!) but thankfully no brimstone! However, of more concern were the similar threats against his next-door neighbour, my tenant Malcolm, who was also my friend. And, from that moment on, the rental payments halved! Thankfully, his tenancy was the new Assured Short-hold Tenancy which had been introduced in 1988 which allowed me to give him 2 months' Notice at the end of the fixed period – which was, by now, up!

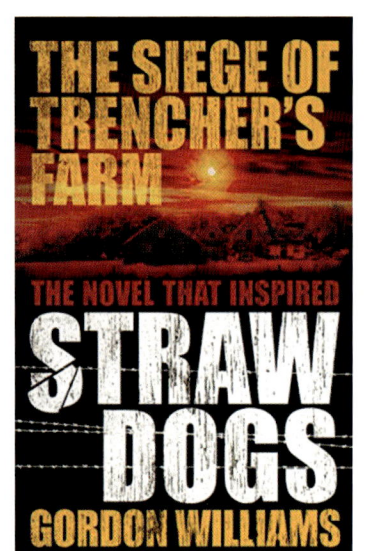

So how did Sylvest enter Mackenzie legend as "The Man with his Stone" ?

Well! by now I had thought my "Straw Dogs" experience of West Cornwall had faded away in the rear view mirror of time but "The Man with his Stone" was up for a sequel! One evening when Sally and I were sitting peacefully at home, in the process of getting ready to go to bed, there was a tremendous bang on one of our double-glazed front windows! We hardly had time to recover from the shock when another and even greater bang occurred. The double-glazing exploded and this time a huge rock landed in our living room along with splinters of glass everywhere! Thankfully neither of us were injured, apart from a cut hand, nor were our pets.

There was then a violent hammering on the back door which Sally bravely answered only to find Sylvest "in his cups" demanding to see me! Rather impolitely Sally declined his request while straining to hold back Wolfy who was intent on loyally executing his guard dog duties. Having been thwarted in their evening's entertainment Sylvest left with his co-attacker and Sally and I called the Police.

After what seemed an age, perhaps an hour, a rather nervous young PC arrived in his panda car, got out slowly and carefully looked round, before knocking on our door. It transpired that Sylvest had previously been convicted of inflicting the same sort of punishment he'd planned for me on another PC. That I am still here to tell the tale is, I am pleased to say, evidence that I did survive this short *Siege of Trencher's Farm*. Never-the-less I did keep a careful lookout for several weeks whenever I went out, especially in the dark.

Fortunately, in a short space of time, we were able to serve Sylvest notice to quit, giving him 2 months to leave my house. As expected, he did not leave on the due date despite challenging the notice in Court and losing, so it became obvious that the bailiffs would have to intervene. When the day of eviction arrived, I took no chances and despite the extra cost, hired two tough looking young builders as my personal "minders", to add to: Sally, myself, the locksmith, two bailiffs and another nervous PC, should there be a breach of the peace, who turned up at the appointed hour.

Sylvest was out when we arrived but soon afterwards, he drove down the track to the cottage. I can still remember the look of astonishment on his face as he got out of his car as he looked at the 8 of us and the 6 extra cars awaiting his arrival! Despite his threats, I almost felt sorry for him… he'd behaved like a raging elephant at times (or maybe a lion?) but he went out like a lamb and Malcolm's new girlfriend immediately moved into the house he'd just vacated, living there happily until they got married several years later.

After a few years I ran into Sylvest again in the builders' merchants and we met each other with the local greeting "all right'n" and decided that what had happened was "all in the past".

Quite soon after that meeting, I was serving on the Planning Committee of Kerrier District Council, when Sylvest indirectly approached me seeking support for his planning application for 2 Local Needs houses he wished to build on the land of the property he had subsequently bought. For some strange reason, the planning officers would only support one extra house in that location rather than two on the basis of "access". Quite honestly, this seemed a nonsensical reason for refusal and the Committee supported his application, as I did! As a result, he rang me and thanked me for my support. Having accepted his thanks, I explained that I did what I considered to be right - and I did! But I'm not sure that he believed me.

Guy and Sally's wedding at Penzance Register Office on 29th February 1996

Sally at Amanda's first wedding in 2007. Behind her are Guy's brother Allan, his wife Robin both obscured by Sally's spectacular hat, and Allan's stepdaughter Heidi

Sally in 1998 with actor and early '60's singing star, John Leyton

Chapter 18
Mackenzie saves Sally, Amanda hits London, Herland Barns completed (Phew!) – 1990

JUST TO PROVE that misfortune comes in threes (first Nancy, then Sylvest), in February Sally became ill. Having endured several operations for Crohn's Disease, she now urgently needed another. The consultant she saw in West Cornwall Hospital reassured her that it was a simple procedure just to cut out another section and join the ends together. It didn't seem simple to me but, being the positive person she is, Sally went into hospital in the belief that in a week or two, she would be well again.

I remember seeing Sally on the day following the operation and her telling me that she had eaten, walked around and was better! But, when the anaesthetic wore off, she was still in severe pain but, nevertheless, was discharged. I'll keep the story short because, quite simply, going into more detail just brings back too much angst for both of us. Within a week she was in Intensive Care for a lifesaving operation! Luckily, the senior surgeon on duty was Martin Mackenzie (no relation) and it was thanks to his skill and abilities that Sally did survive. I was absolutely distraught and I especially remember speaking at length to my mother and, for once, pouring out my heart to her. However, her kindness and understanding at my time of need did reassure me that, with Sally's determination and strength of character, all would be well.

Sally still had a long, hard and painful road ahead which she bravely endured but it was about a year before she was stitched back together again! However, it was another 8 years before a 2 month stay in the Radcliffe Hospital, Oxford which, involved another serious operation before she became completely well again.

While Sally was in Oxford, Amanda who had, by now, moved to London came and visited her as often as she could as did Lucy who was, at that time, living in Hampshire

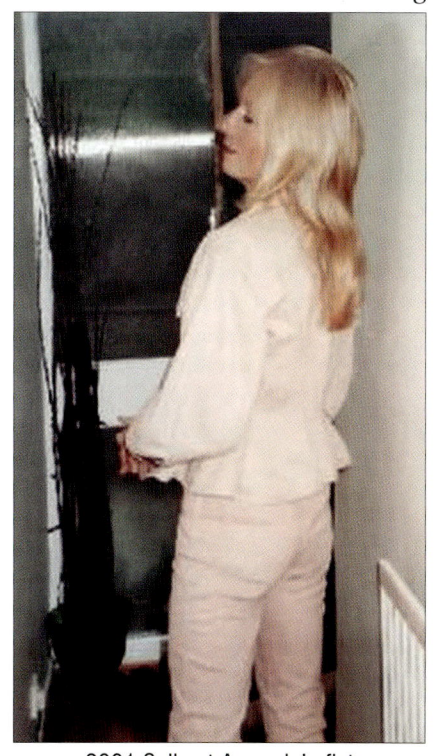

2001 Sally at Amanda's flat

and neither Sally nor I will ever forget the time and support they gave her when she needed it most.

Now back to 1990 and this was the year that Amanda, aged 18, decided to try out London! My friend Martin Kennedy-Bell who was by now enjoying a bachelor lifestyle which involved snooker, cards with his friends and nights out, offered that she could stay in one of his spare rooms for a month. Poor Martin (or should I say Amanda) had no concept of what would be involved in having a teenager stay in his home or, for that matter, could Amanda have anticipated from the alternative perspective. If football was on, then Amanda (who hated football) had to forget her favourite "soap" and watch *Match of the Day*. And if she was out when Martin's mother came to clean his house, his mother always forgot that Amanda didn't have a second key for the mortise lock so Amanda was locked out till Martin came home whatever time that might be. So let's just say that the first 3 weeks were challenging for all concerned! But one bright spot in that time was when our cousin, Alistair (Lord) Kilmarnock invited Amanda for tea in the House of Lords. And later, she got to know the family who, it has to be said, were somewhat eccentric! At that time, Alistair was living with his wife Hilary in the basement of Kingsley Amis' house. Kingsley had been Hilary's first husband, and as the newspaper gossip columns papers kept reminding everybody, Alistair was employed as Kingsley's butler!

However, by the last week, Amanda was starting to enjoy London partly as she got a job as a teaching assistant at a school in London's East End which she was not only very good at but she loved it too. Of course they wanted her to stay on but, when her month was up, she came back to Cornwall although by then she had decided that London was where she wanted to live. Soon after she returned with her friend Jessica and has lived in London ever since.

During her last week Martin took pity on Amanda's staying in every night, and invited her to one of the several singles events he helped organise. Of course an attractive, vivacious 18 year old girl finding herself thrust into a party atmosphere with everyone else, at the very least, twice her age (or maybe quite a lot more) made her the star of the evening! Everyone made a fuss of her and, Martin told me several years later, that people who were there on that night, for years afterwards, kept asking about Amanda. Quite a few of those people were, unsurprisingly, men but none turned her head.

However the evening threw up a new challenge for Amanda as it turned out that Martin did have an ulterior motive for inviting her. The evening happened to be Martin's drinking night and, when they left, Martin gave Amanda the keys to his car and asked her to drive them home! Poor Amanda, who had already had a couple of drinks herself (just to steady her nerves) had only just passed her driving test in a tiny Nissan Micra car and in rural Cornwall too. She'd never driven in London and never driven Martin's car. It was an almost new and very smart Rover, nor did she have a clue how to get back to Chiswick. Martin wasn't any help either. To quote Chuck Berry he was "feelin' no pain" – an expression which, in this case – might be the understatement of the year! Somehow, and nobody knows quite how, they did eventually get back to Martin's house and the car was in one piece too! – despite a few crunchy gear changes. An unforgettable evening but thankfully a safe one and, for the record, Martin and Amanda are still friends.

Back in Cornwall, I applied to alter the Planning Permission for the small single storey barn at Herland Farm from a workshop to a dwelling. The Planning Department in their wisdom (?) recommended refusal despite the fact that the Estate Agents couldn't find any prospective buyers for a workshop. Thankfully the Planning Committee decided that Consent should be granted! However,"Jimmy" Dann the Chief Planning Officer wasn't going to have his recommendation entirely thwarted and he persuaded the Committee to agree that a Section 52 obligation should be attached to the Consent which removed the right to extend the property, or build within its cartilage, at any future time. Well that was better than nothing! But nothing could surpass the inefficiency of Kerrier District Council's legal department as the binding agreement they sent me to sign, prior to issuing the written documentation, listed my home address as the address of the Barn! Of course, I signed as required but made a mental note to appeal at a later date if I subsequently decided to extend the property!

With the memories of forgetful Bingo, bolshie MB and the resulting aggravation of Barn No.1 still fresh in my mind, I decided to employ a small firm of local builders to undertake this conversion. Their work progressed satisfactorily (Hooray), was completed on time and resulted in the attractive barn conversion one can see today which still forms part of our property portfolio. And, as a bonus, this single storey roof only had to be slated once (Ahem! Ahem!). As a result, for all of the 30+ houses I've built since then, rather than using a "rag, tag and bobtail" of the good, the bad and the truly incompetent, I've always employed similar small local firms of professional builders who have proved to be better, no more expensive and, as a result, far less stressful for me.

> **Postscript**: Several years later, I did challenge the validity of the Section 52 and Kerrier District Council had no option but to agree that the obligation wasn't enforceable and, as a result, granted consent for not just one but, subsequently, two extensions!

The small single story barn at Herland Farm showing one of the extensions and part of the other

Wheal Buller Count House before it was redeveloped

Chapter 19
The Wonderful World of Cornish Property
1991 – 2022

AS ANYONE of a certain age involved with property will remember, after the property boom of the late 1980s, there followed the bust of the 1990s which lasted till the early Naughties. I had ridden the boom but with the ongoing construction of the first couple of houses on the land at Herland Farm (Heriand Parc) and the conversion of the small barn at Herland Farm, cash was in very short supply. Then I saw a huge ruin with 2 acres of land near Redruth for sale by auction – it was what was left of the (Account) Count House and Mine Captain's House of the once fabulously profitable (in the 1800s) Wheal Buller Mine and it had the questionable benefit of a Demolition Order which had been served in the 1960s! Guide price? Just £3-4,000!

I just had to try and buy it so I spoke to my bank manager. Back in the day you could do that! We agreed a budget of £4,000 with a top-up for the property later, for stabilisation and planning applications. Come the day I found myself bidding against a local contractor who wanted to demolish it for the stone but I got it for £4,250. Then! With the help of my sister, Lucy, it took me nearly three years to obtain planning permission for two dwellings. After which, with the financial encouragement of my mother, who came to live with us in 1994, I sold it.

After another change of ownership, a family of builders recreated this fabulous and historic building and still own it today. The full history can be found in my website. Search online for "The Wheal Buller Project".

After I sold Wheal Buller. I started looking around for inexpensive properties to add to our growing property portfolio which had temporarily stalled. Due to the property crash there were plenty. Fortunately, because Sally and I had assets, two friendly bank managers, one after the other, were only too happy to give us 100% loans (base rate + 2%) on properties which cost as little as £8,000. Over the next few years we built up quite a portfolio in the Camborne, Redruth area, utilising all the rent to pay off the loans as quickly as possible. Then having paid off our loans, we then upgraded with replacement windows, doors, new kitchens and bathrooms.

We also bought a smallholding near our home, which had been rented by some friends for 40 years. Their landlord suddenly decided to sell but sought to evict them first! Consequently we replaced the roof and windows and they stayed for another 10 years at the same rent they'd previously been paying which was just £100 per month. We obtained planning consent for the barn which came with the farmhouse and it has now been stunningly converted by our friends, Jim and Linda Taylor, almost entirely on their own! After they brought it from us.

Over the years we had bought and sold properties and land but it was in the 1980s that I first heard of Goynes Field. My ex, Paulene, had bought a couple of holiday caravans there. It was a very run down holiday park situated a few hundred yards from Porthtowan beach just behind what was locally referred to as the "Ghetto". It comprised about 30 units, mainly holiday chalets most of which were little more than garden sheds – with or without facilities!, and an assortment of about 25 caravans, in varying states of disrepair, including a converted charabanc! None of the owners had security of tenure so I decided to monitor the site in case it came up for sale.

In 1992 it did! Fed up with the drinking, drugs and non-payment of ground rent the owner had simply had enough and put the site up for sale along with about 12 acres of land. I tried to buy it but the owner wouldn't sell unless the purchaser had experience of running a similar business. Fortunately, I knew someone who did, Leigh Ibbotson, and together with our wives we bought and renamed it Tregoyne. Our first move was to double the ground rent although there were, of course, some protests! In return we promised to upgrade the park with tarmac roads and parking areas, low level street lighting and the employment of an on site warden to undertake maintenance which, over a short period of time, was exactly what we did!

From the beginning, we upgraded all the chalets we owned and rented them out until the park was redeveloped. But life at Tregoyne certainly wasn't always easy in the early days. We had to do a certain amount of "sorting out" of existing owners and some of our new tenants too including a "working girl" who's phone never seemed to stop ringing day or night – much to the annoyance of her nearest neighbours! Meanwhile, we applied for planning consent for 30 dwellings in the chalet area and, a few years later, this application was approved. Consequently over the next 20 or so years, we built all the properties, almost always on a "build one – sell one basis" as we completed the development. This meant there was no need to borrow money after we'd paid off our initial loan.

In due course we applied for permission to redevelop the caravan area with holiday homes and this was eventually approved in 2009. However, by now, the Ibbotsons had grown tired of my desire never to borrow money and wanted to finance this new development in one go! A parting of the ways was inevitable and after 5 months of negotiation (or was it a psychological warfare?) we went our separate ways, splitting the assets 50/50 although Sally and I kept the Company which has, only once in 30 years, recorded a loss. Well OK! My daughters will confirm that I am a typical Scot – tight! But, all our family will benefit one day.

Today with all the dwellings built, along with 26 holiday homes and, as I understand it more to come (time will tell!), Tregoyne is almost unrecognisable from what it had been all those years ago and now it's the "in place" to live in Porthtowan!

One final memory of Tregoyne involved our property there. In early 1991 Sally bought her first horse, Wooky. Due to her long stay in hospital that year, she decided to loan him to a riding school for the summer on condition he was insured and cared for by the school. The school was a franchise at Haven Holidays, Perranporth run by a man called Quentin Duckett Blacke (QDB). Wooky was due to be returned to us on my birthday – the day that everything seems to happen to me! Our friends, Caroline and Will Hoddinott with their two children Amy (11) and Matt (9) came for the day. However, when QDB arrived at our house, there was no horse! He explained that there had been an accident and Wooky had broken his leg after he'd lost a shoe and had been destroyed! Sally was distraught and could barely believe what we'd been told. I asked about the insurance but QDB admitted that he hadn't insured Wooky and couldn't afford to repay us anything! Whereupon I "lost the plot" and, as a result, QDB had to make an unscheduled visit to A&E in Helston hospital! He was diagnosed as suffering from concussion.

Several days later I had "my collar felt", and in due course, ended up in Court charged with ABH. Our friends, The Hoddinotts, attended with us for moral support. I will never forget 11 year old Amy – now a very successful vet with two practices and property developer as well! – saying to my solicitor: "I didn't see Guy hitting him and I'm happy to stand up and say that"! And, she would have done! Of course my solicitor wouldn't allow her to act as a witness due to her age. The outcome was that I now had a criminal conviction and had to pay QDB, compensation for his injuries.

However, Sally and I then sued QDB in the County Court and won! I then contacted the owners of Haven Holidays – and who was the Rank Director responsible for the holiday parks? It was none other than Angus Crighton-Miller, the son of my headmaster when I was at Stowe. In due course QDB lost his franchise!

Tregoyne was involved because following the loss of his riding franchise Quentin Duckett Blacke subsequently submitted a planning application for a riding school at Porthtowan but his chosen ride, unbelievably, utilised the road leading to Tregoyne! And, who owned that road? We did!? Consequently we objected and his application was refused!

I shall finish this chapter as I began it, with a ruined Count House! The first one was big but this one is definitely small, although even more historic. It was the original Count House which served Ding Dong Mine. It was at Ding Dong then known as Ting Tong Mine, where in 1797, the famous Cornish engineer Richard Trevithick, undertook his first experiments with high pressure steam. It was steam powered pumps which pumped the water out of the mines to stop them flooding. In doing so he broke the Boulton & Watt patent and, as a result was served with an injunction which was, no doubt, posted on the door of this building. However this giant of a man "threatened to throw anyone who tried to stop him down the (mine) shaft!"

I bought the building with nearly an acre of land (and it has fabulous views towards Mounts Bay and St Michael's Mount) expecting to get planning consent to rebuild it exactly as it would have looked around the time Richard Trevithick would have known it. But, so far, no luck!

Surely it's day will come; especially as it is situated within the Cornish Mining World Heritage site and because, this Count House – with its association to Richard Trevithick – is one of the most important buildings associated with the Industrial Revolution!

Wheal Buller Count House after redevelopment

Guy on his Norton Jubilee Twin with his dogs: Bruno (left); Gemma, the rottweiler he rescued and Wolfie. Pictured in 1990

Chapter 20
Glimpses into the Life of a Local Politician!
1991 – 2003

THE LAND that came as a "make weight" with the Barns at Herland Farm seemed an obvious possibility for development. So I decided to try and obtain planning consent. However, there was a difficulty. Situated considerably outside the curtilage of Godolphin village, the land only seemed a possibility for a "local needs housing development". This was a policy recently introduced by Kerrier District Council which allowed development to be approved, outside but adjacent to the designated boundaries of settlements provided the houses were occupied by first time buyers from the local area. So, I was concerned that my plans would not meet the new policy requirements.

I'd heard of the late Pam Lyne, who was a Parish, Kerrier District and Cornwall County councillor, as someone who would fight for local people! So I rang her and asked for her help. She was, then, a striking lady who, although she'd been born in Oxfordshire, had a strong Cornish accent having married into a large local farming family. By chance the family owned farms and land adjoining Frenchman's Creek made famous by Daphne Du Maurier's novel of the same name and a favourite walk of mine.

Pam, as the saying goes, was "once met, never forgotten". She was full of confidence and always strode around in skin tight trousers and wrestling boots.. Her "style" seemed very appropriate as she was a real fighter for what she believed in and, thankfully, she believed in my proposed development! I managed to obtain planning consent for 6 houses, which I subsequently built.

It was during our discussions that Pam convinced me that I should stand for election as a Parish and District Councillor in the elections due in 1991. Pam was an Independent and, therefore, not aligned to any political party and this seemed the obvious political affiliation for me, and for the next 12 years local politics became a huge part of my life.

In 1991 I put my name forward for Germoe Parish Council and Kerrier District Council but was beaten into third place, for the latter, by local businessman Alan Johns and Terrye Jones, now Lady Teverson, following her marriage to the Lib Dem peer, Lord Teverson in 2006. Back then she had been recruited by the Lib Dems to stand as their Parliamentary candidate for the Falmouth and Camborne constituency. In fact, over time, she unsuccessfully contested three general elections.

It was at a by-election, 2 years later when Alan stood down, that proved to be the real start of my career in local politics as I was then elected to Kerrier District

Council. Over that 12 year period I stood for election, in total, 5 times – winning 4 and, in the last in 1999, substantially beating Terrye Jones into 2nd place! I finally called it a day and stood down in 2003. In the meantime, between 1992 and 1999, I also served as a Member of Breage Parish Council.

Germoe Parish Council is a small rural parish with a population of just over 400 residents and, quite honestly, very little of note ever happened there. However, I do remember, quite soon after I was elected, hearing about a group of unruly "travellers" who had taken up residence on Greenbury Downs. The local couple who lived nearby were distraught and begged the Parish Council to help get their new neighbours evicted. The chairman of the Council was reluctant to get involved so I fought their corner, winning a resolution to take the necessary legal action. Unsurprisingly, I and the Parish Council clerk, drew the short straw and had to serve the travellers Notice to Leave! Thankfully we both survived, despite the obvious alcohol and drug abuse on display, duly served the Notice and, surprise, surprise, they left on the following day!

I also recall during the time when I was Chairman that I faced a vote of "no confidence" but I can't remember why! Although it might have been because I invited our then Lib Dem MP, Andrew George, to attend one of our meetings. The vote was close run but, of course, I voted for myself and won the day!

Finally, I remember a gypsy couple who bought a field in the Parish and subsequently applied for planning permission to base their caravan there. They asked me for my help as Kerrier District Council planned to refuse their application. Fortunately, all their near neighbours supported them, as did I, and their application was unanimously approved. By then I was also member of Kerrier District Council's Planning Committee that also supported them, despite the "howls" of protest from the then Chief Planning Officer, "Jimmy" Dann – I still don't know why! A few days afterwards. I found a small basket of ducks eggs left on my doorstep, as a thank you for my support!

Breage Parish Council served the villages of Breage, Ashton. Godolphin, Praa Sands and Carleen and was a much more challenging Council. There were some quite bitter arguments at our meetings with subsequent falling outs, but we all managed to make friends afterwards at the Queens Arms pub in Breage, buying each other drinks until closing time or even beyond! (Many years later I played there with 2 different bands.)

I remember that each of us had the responsibility to check whether the street lights were working in each area of the Parish where we lived. Every month we'd report the failed lights and the Parish Council clerk would tell us that she'd write to the electricity board (I think it was SWEB at that time) to get them repaired. Every month it seemed that the same ones still wouldn't work and, when asked, the clerk used to say: "I wrote but haven't heard anything"! So one month a fellow councillor, Ken Babbage, and I, in exasperation decided to do a survey of the Parish street lights! We found that nearly half (16 if I recall correctly!) weren't working. We wrote our own letter and, within a month, all lights were doing what a street light has to do! If I recall correctly, it wasn't long afterwards that the

Monday July 15 1996

Leisure hits top profit at £70,000

A RECORD profit of over £70,000 has been reported by the Kerrier Council department which is responsible for running the authority's leisure facilities.

Cllr Guy Mackenzie (Ind, Breage), who is chairman of Kerrier's Direct Services Board, has paid tribute to the staff who have succeeded in reversing the fortunes at Carn Brea leisure centre, Helston sports centre, Tuckingmill pavilion and Helston's Coronation Lake and park.

Following two years in which losses totalled £130,000, he said the excellent results had been achieved through a number of rationalisation measures aimed at improving efficiency and by financial streamlining.

The profit made during the past year has allowed the leisure department to hand back £20,000 to Kerrier's amenities committee so that the money can be ploughed back into providing additional services.

Kerrier Direct Services, the council's contracting arm, made an overall surplus of £173,000 during the past 12 months.

It represents a significant increase on the previous year and equates to a larger profit than the total for all the other years that KDS has been operating.

Cllr Mackenzie explained that much of the surplus would be handed back to the council for investment in district-wide projects, with the housing committee receiving £40,000 and the environmental services committee getting £20,000.

Parish Council clerk did the decent thing and resigned!

The big issues in the parish always seemed to concern Praa Sands. Someone once said that this village alone took up about 80% of every meeting! Looking back they always seemed to involve people who'd retired to this lovely area with its sea views, bought a bungalow and when they'd completed the redesign of their property and gardens, found themselves with nothing to do. So they subsequently fell out with their neighbours or mostly, with one of the local businesses. Then they tried to get the Parish Council involved.

The biggest issue was the parking of cars on part of the village green which overlooked the sea and the charges that the combative owner charged for this privilege. Actually there should have been no parking on this village green anyway! This battle was raging when I became a member in 1992 and continued after I resigned in 1999, although, just before, I'd been the proposer of a motion that the Council take legal action against the owner. Some time afterwards, in the early 2000s, the matter came to Court. The Council won and legal costs of (as I recall) £75,000 awarded in their favour! Today the matter is settled with 3 car parks in the area and there's no parking on the village green!

As for Kerrier District Council, honestly? I could write a book on my 10 years as an elected Member of KDC (as it was known) but would anyone read it? I don't think so! So I'll just pick out a few memories which, hopefully, won't bore you, dear reader!

The Council was under no political overall control. When I was first elected it was run by a coalition of Independents and Lib Dems. Following the elections of 1995, it was subject to a coalition of Labour and Independents. From my point of view, I preferred working with the Labour Party. They were open to new ideas and loyal unlike the Conservatives who were, well, too conservative and always went along with the recommendations of the Council officers (as they liked to style themselves!) As for some of the Lib Dems, they always seemed to be scheming for something or other… but I'm not sure if they always knew what! The Independents, well they (and I!) were just independent!

Despite the fact that members make decisions and officers merely carry them out, it seemed to me that the Council was effectively controlled by two megalithic departments, Planning and Environmental Health, and neither the 'twain would meet'. However, I have to admit that this had worked in my favour in the 1980s when the Planning Department had refused my planning applications for Treskillard whereas, in direct contrast. Environmental Health approved 90% Council grants for the modernisation of both properties!

Never-the-less the Committee which I enjoyed the most was the Planning Committee. It was really interesting. I learnt a lot but always enjoyed the "knockabouts" which Madam Chairman, Pam Lyne, had with the then Chief Planning Officer, Jimmy Dann. I can still remember him, in exasperation during one meeting, saying in public: "If you had your way Mrs Lyne, you'd have a line of houses all the way from Helston to the Lizard!" Pam Lyne's reply was: "If I had my way Mr. Dann, I'd have a line of houses all the way from Redruth to Helston and onto the Lizard and they'd all be for local people!" Touche!

One memory of a planning site meeting, which sticks in my mind, is the one in which the local member enthusiastically supported a planning application in public session with the applicants present. But as soon as we went into private session, immediately proposed refusal! It was in fact refused, but, no doubt, he told the applicants, when the decision had been made public, that he'd done everything he could to get it approved! That was his way but he will, nevertheless, remain nameless!

The really big issue for me and the Council was the story of the Leisure Contract. John Major's Conservative Government of the early 1990s decided that some council functions had to go to Compulsive Competitive tender (CCT) but in-house teams were allowed to tender for them too. Thankfully the Leisure Contract and the Building Contracts, known as Kerrier Direct Services (KDS), had been won by the in-house team.

In 1995, I was elected Chairman of the Direct Services Board (DSB) which managed both Contracts. When I took over, the building division was just profitable but, the "star of the show", was the Leisure Contract which controlled all the Council's leisure facilities. However, within a few weeks, the Council's treasurer (who was responsible for the accounts for both) reported that there had been a mistake in the accounts and that the Leisure Contract had, in fact, lost around £130,000 in the last two years!

The DSB immediately set up a working party to investigate these losses and quite soon we found apparent evidence of incompetence and fraud. We then put new rules and guidelines in place and replaced the managers of both Helston & Carn Brea Leisure Centres and set about making the Leisure Contract profitable.

Within about 18 months this had been achieved with a profit of £70,000 and KDS did even better declaring a surplus of £173,000. The DSB then decided to do something that had seldom been done since CCT had been introduced, to actually hand back a share of the profits (in total £80,000) to our client, Kerrier District Council!

Storm clouds were on the horizon for the DSB as the powers that be in the Council and the District Auditor (who had signed off the incorrect Leisure Contract accounts!) confirmed that the Leisure Contract had to be re-tendered, despite the profits it was now making. But, the DSB was not declared the winner of the new Contract and a handover was expected shortly afterwards.

Fearing for their jobs, the Leisure staff were unhappy about this decision, as were the Labour council members, some Independents and a few Lib Dems, not forgetting many residents of Kerrier district as well.

Also scrutiny of the tendered costs did not seem, to the DSB, to stack up financially. So the battle of the Leisure Contract began! It raged on for about two years and help was given in this fight by the future Labour Government which was, until 1997, still in opposition and I still have correspondence to confirm this.

However, the day came when the Council were served a Section 114 Report which gave no option but to hand over the contract to the winning bidder! Then the Audit Commission intervened, they declared that, by not handing over the Contract previously, the Council had acted unlawfully and thus cost the taxpayers extra.

Consequently a major investigation was undertaken by the Audit Commission. I was interviewed three times and, my friend Martin Kennedy-Bell, who had a law degree, kindly accompanied me on each occasion. The report was published in 1999, coincidentally on my birthday! I, along with Pam Lyne (by then Chairman of Finance), Amenities Committee Chairman, Steven Barnes, the Chief Executive and the Treasurer were all criticised but none of us were found guilty of "wilful misconduct"! We'd all done what we thought was in the best interests of the taxpayers of Kerrier District!

And the winner was!.. the Audit Commission who charged the residents and taxpayers of Kerrier over £250.000 for their services! Several years later Prime Minister David Cameron's coalition government abolished the Audit Commission as it had "lost its way."

In a speech to the Full Council on 27th May 1997, I had ended by saying "…one day a new DSB will successfully reclaim the Leisure contract". And, one day, to a great extent, they did!

Ask Audit Commission to repay wasted money

I READ with interest the decision of the coalition Government, reported in the national press on Saturday, August 14, to abolish the Audit Commission.

In his statement, the Communities Secretary, Eric Pickles, was quoted as saying: "The corporate centre of the Audit Commission has lost its way."

The press also quoted critics who "had long claimed that the Audit Commission went far beyond its brief of ensuring value for money".

I recall that in 1999, the district auditor investigated Kerrier District Council's leisure contract; also the delay of the award of that contract to an alternative contractor.

In an apparently confused and confusing 140-page report, which cost taxpayers more than £250,000, several senior officers and members of the council, serving at that time, were strongly criticised.

However, the report surprisingly failed either to substantially apportion criticism to members of the committee, or its chairman, which delayed making the decision to award the contract!

Nor did it include any research (other than one sentence!) of the very concerns, identified by the Direct Services Board, which helped instigate the investigation in the first place!

No doubt there are many others apart from me who not only agree with the sentiments as reported but also consider that the Audit Commission had "lost its way" some considerable time ago!

Of course I'd like to congratulate my (very distant) cousin David Cameron, and our Government, for making this decision a part of their cost-cutting measures.

But I'd also like to ask whether this report could be revisited and, if found deficient as suggested, the Audit Commission could be asked, prior to its demise, to repay the taxpayers' money, which has apparently been wasted.

GUY MACKENZIE
Ashton

Guy's letter to the press on the demise of the Audit Commission

The best part of me being a councillor, well certainly for Sally anyway, were the Christmas parties with wives/girlfriends/partners invited. These were held in the Members Room at the Council Offices in Camborne. There was always a generous supply of food and drink! Of course, the Conservatives were, well conservative, in their consumption of either and left early. The Lib Dems more relaxed (liberal?) with their consumption, the Independents were... independent, but it was the Labour Members (especially Mark Jeffery, Ron and Colin Godolphin) who knew how to enjoy themselves.

Everyone made a fuss of Sally, not least because she was more outspoken than most, to say the least! But Sally especially remembers one Independent Member who was known as being a "trencherman" (who must remain anonymous) eating an entire pudding which was meant to serve twelve! He was a very pleasant chap who, unsurprisingly, has long since passed away and at a young age too.

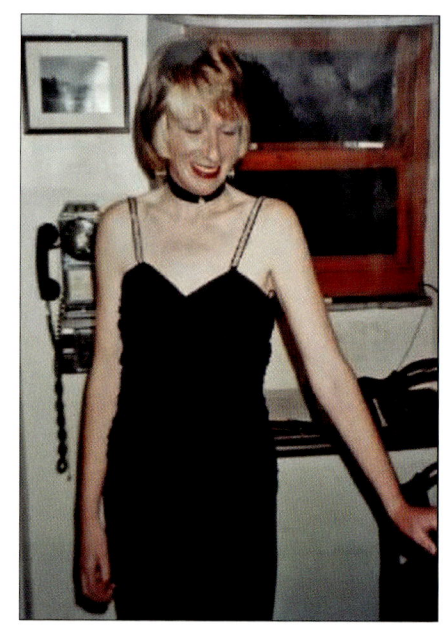

1993 Sally off to the Helston Mayor's Ball

Speech made at Kerrier District Council Full Council Meeting 27th May 1997

Madam Chairman,

As Chairman of Direct Services I've asked to speak first.

May I immediately say that, following the issuing of the Section 114 Report, this Council has no realistic alternative but to Note the Report and award the Leisure Contract to Relaxion.

This is without doubt the hardest statement I have ever made in this Chamber.

Madam Chairman can you or any Member of this Council who was not here in 1994 begin to understand what the Direct Services Board, the Leisure Staff and the Unions have achieved over the last 3 years?

In 1994 this Contract was losing EIGHT THOUSAND POUNDS EVERY MONTH and was a disaster for the taxpayers of Kerrier.

But in September of that year, against the advice of the Chief Services Officer (Mr J Cadman) nearly every Member of the Council voted to back the previous Board under the excellent Chairmanship of Councillor Sid Godolphin to try and sort it out.

That confidence has been fully justified and through sheer hard work, co-operation and sound business practices, the Leisure Contract has been transformed into one which consistently makes a profit every month and has even returned money to its Client Committee! That profit has not been achieved by deferring maintenance and I've written to Hilary Armstrong on that point.

For the Direct Services Board, the Staff and the Members who have consistently backed us -to lose the Contract now is a bitter, bitter disappointment.

Before I finish I'd like to ask some questions:

Firstly, I understand that Post Tender negotiations are contrary to the European Services Directive is this correct?

Secondly, it has been reported by the Treasurer and minuted that the Direct Services Board could run this Contract on the Original Contract terms and price tendered of £339,000 plus inflation. A total of around £354,000. At face value this appears to be less than Relaxion's latest tender of £367,000 plus extras and including the almost immediate installation of their own Health Suite or compensation in lieu. Is this correct? However, I understand that there is a binding Contract between this Council and our existing Health Suite Supplier which cannot be terminated until next year. If so, what is the real first year cost of Relaxion's tendered price, and is this within this Council's budget?

Finally, if this Contract is awarded to Relaxion today, as I feel that it will, may I on behalf of the Direct Services Board, ask them to protect all the Services on offer, may I seek that they cherish our staff they are the best - and may I wish them success in their temporary stewardship, because one day a new Direct Services Board will successfully reclaim the Leisure Contract - ONE DAY THE D.S.B. WILL BE BACK!!

Kerrier District Councillor Guy Mackenzie
Meeting of Breage Parish Council, 1st April 2003

Farewell Speech

Mr Chairman,

It probably hasn't escaped the attention of anyone here tonight that next month there will be two new Kerrier District Councillors representing this new Ward, Breage/Germoe which is now included with Crowan at Kerrier District Council.

As you know I have served as District Councillor for Breage & Germoe parishes for 10 years and have been a Parish Councillor for 12 years which includes 8 years on this Parish Council. In that time I have been involved in five elections, four of which I have won. But while it was never my intention to spend the rest of my life in local politics, my decision not to seek re-election this year was made simply because my business commitments have taken off recently in a way that I never anticipated all those years ago.

Now I don't want to take up too much of this Council's valuable time tonight but as this is my last Ordinary Meeting of Breage Parish Council as your Kerrier District Councillor, I would like to make mention of a few highlights and a lowlight of the last few years.

With regard to this Council I'm delighted that the court case at Praa Sands is now resolved - not least (and it seems "forever" ago!) that I recall that I was the Proposer of that motion!

On a Kerrier level I have been pleased to be involved in the dismantling of two megalithic departments (Planning and Services) and their replacement by the new Management Structure which has resulted in better relationships between Officers, Members and the residents of Kerrier, AND more accountability, which is a benefit to all.

I was also proud during my time as Chairman of Kerrier Direct Services to be part of a team which not only achieved record surpluses but also made enough profit to be able to hand back substantial amounts of money to each of our three Client Committees, something that has very rarely happened in the history of CCT (Compulsory Competitive Tendering).

At the same time, the fortunes of the loss-making Kerrier Leisure Contract were transformed into a surplus of nearly £100,000. I would make mention that although the District Auditor at one time didn't consider that that contract should have remained in-house (unlike some members of the present Government who were in opposition at that time - and not a lot of people know that!) most people now accept that subsequent events and experience have demonstrated that that would have been the best way forward for the Council.

However, the time I enjoyed most has been my 8 years as a Member of Kerrier Planning Committee and my involvement with a lot of Planning issues, many involving this Parish.

Finally I'm pleased that Kerrier Council's finances have turned out so satisfactorily from a low of 18 months ago and in a tight financial situation, to set a Council Tax – increase of only 5% compared to up about, for example, 39% for the Police Authority, is a remarkable result for Kerrier District Council - for confirmation of this just look at the rises across the U.K

I'd also like to mention some of the personalities I've been involved with over the last 10-12 years.

Firstly, my Co-District Councillor, Terrye Jones (now Terrye Teverson). She was always competitive which was good for me because she kept me on my toes. I'll always remember her as a first class, off the cuff, public speaker and a powerful ally in the battles we've fought together. I wish her well in her new venture into Ladies "smalls" (underwear). Unfortunately her prices are way beyond my means - but my wife lives in hopes!

I'd also like to pay a tribute to David Roberts (our Cornwall County Councillor) who was a highly respected "elder statesman" when I was just a "trainee" and now is still a highly regarded elder statesman. The only annoying thing is that he doesn't look a day older!

I'd also like to mention Rod Coward, who in the early days of his Clerkship at Germoe Parish Council, helped me a lot and on a personal basis too. Now that he is once again off on his travels, I'd just like to wish him the best for the future and say that I hope he finds whatever it is that he's looking for. Finally I'd like to pay a tribute to Tony Woodhams – we haven't always agreed but that's as it should be after all – if there was no politicising in politics there would be no need for politicians! (Please don't anyone say that the world would be a better place for that!). But I'll particularly remember Tony as being highly organised, a first class administrator and certainly the best chairman of Breage Parish Council I've known. I wish him the best for the future. I'd finally like to remember the late Bob Parker who got me into Politics all those years ago and Alan and Barbara Johns without whose help I'd probably never have been elected.

Last, but certainly not least, I'd like to thank my wife for putting up with all the phone calls, the late night meetings, the support she's always given me and especially just for "being there". Thank you, Sally.

Mr Chairman, it's been a great privilege to serve this community as your Kerrier District Councillor and I wish the two new Councillors the enjoyment I've had. From what I know of them I believe that they will both be a credit to this Parish and if either if them at any time feel I can be of assistance, please call me.

In closing, Id just like to say that there are many things I shall miss as I go into "retirement" from local politics – not least the many good friends I have made and also councillor Mick Clayton (Kerrier District Council, cabinet member) who is here tonight and has been a good friend of this Parish. Also I'd particularly like to thank everyone who voted for me – without you I wouldn't be here – and I just hope that I lived up to your expectations. To those who didn't, I just hope that you feel that I've given you the fair hearing and support I've tried to give anyone seeking my help. That has always been my aim for everyone.

There's an old saying "parting is such sweet sorrow" – and it is, but it's also time for me to move on and as I do I'd just like to say again, it's a privilege to serve a community such as ours and I envy my successors that privilege. But, Mr Chairman, it's been MY PRIVILEGE to serve this community for the last 10 years.

Guy and Ron Barrett at the Camborne Conservative Club in 2012

The Ron Barrett Trio with Ron (left) Guy on his drums and Andy Pascoe

Chapter 21
Back on the Road Again
2012 – 2016

I HUNG UP MY DRUMSTICKS in 1989, packed my drums away and never expected to play music again. but along came Ron Barrett who'd been a professional guitarist through the '70s and '80s. I'd met him thanks to my guitar website and he wanted me to back him and friends at a Charity Concert in Camborne Conservative Club. I resisted his first offer but he persisted and on 5th November 2012 I was "back on the road again" with, surprisingly, a full house and a very enthusiastic audience!

So hooked again in 2013, I was off to a jam session held by Alan (Al) Rideout and his partner KC (Cassandra) Johnson which I thoroughly enjoyed. Over the next few months I played anywhere I could to get back "in the groove" and, in August, joined the Parchman Blues Band led by local businessman, John Cowles. Our first gig was at a festival on top of the cliffs overlooking Looe which was great fun but I soon tired of the rather dreary flow of blues music, and all sung by John as he carefully read the words of each song as he strummed his guitar!

One amusing recollection was John telling us that his rather prim wife had been so shocked at the lyrics of one song that she asked her husband to stop playing it, when she finally realised the meaning! It was of one of our most popular numbers *Dust my Broom* by Elmore James: "I'm getting up soon in the mornin', I believe I'll dust my broom…"

And, not content with just one band, in November, I joined ex-show jumper and Rock 'n' Roller', Ben Davis & The Thunderbirds! They had a huge set list but, at every rehearsal, Ben always insisted on trying out new numbers rather than perfecting the existing ones. When I mentioned this to guitarist Chris Ward, he said: "Oh don't worry, we do a different version every time we play our set!"

However we did have some fun gigs and I remember especially the first at the Red Jackets pub in Camborne where we finished at nearly 1 am as the audience insisted that we carried on as, unsurprisingly, did the landlord! Also, a Festival gig at Mawla near Porthtowan to which Amanda and Ian, my future son-in-law, came as they'd done previously on New Year's Eve when I was with the Parchman Blues Band.

But, not content with two bands (neither ideally suited me), I formed the Al Rideout Band in January 2014 with Al and KC and, later, keyboard player Simon Bowman joined us for several gigs. Our most enjoyable were at the Queens Arms in Breage which had served me so well following the Breage Parish Council Meetings, all those years a go!

The Guy Mackenzie Trio with KC Johnson (left) Guy on Drums and Al Rideout

US legend Charlie Gracie playing with the Ron Barrett Trio at the Godolphin Club in 2014

But I wanted more, and having amicably parted with both John Cowles and Ben Davis, I looked around for a "name" to play music with. And I found USA legend Charlie Gracie on his annual tour of the UK (his first UK tour was in 1958!) and with dates to fill! His 1950s Chart topping hits, *Butterfly*, *Fabulous* etc., were also recorded by Cliff Richard, Paul McCartney, Andy Williams, Tommy Steele etc., etc.

So, having arranged a date with Charlie's agent, I next had to secure a venue, put a band together and, of course, sell the tickets! With the Godolphin Club in Helston booked as the venue, the obvious choice for guitarist was Ron Barrett as Charlie had always been Ron's idol and he even owned a Guild guitar almost identical to Charlie's! Ron then persuaded his friend, Andy Pascoe, who owned Modern Music in Truro, to join us on bass calling ourselves The Ron Barrett Trio.

I subsequently decided to make the event a Charity Concert in aid of Cornwall Air Ambulance Trust and, as supporting performers, we secured the a-capella ladies No Apologies which included our friends. Penny Whittle & her daughter Sara Tripconey singing '50s and '60s numbers Also, our friend John Roskruge's band, The Pistoleros, who played their versions of R&B standards and 1960s classics. Legendary Cornish DJ Freddy Zapp. enthusiastically agreed to compere the show assisted by BBC South West's Matt Shepherd. The stage was set.

The evening was a fabulous success and the Concert was a sell out which raised over £2,000 for the Charity! As people, Charlie and his wife Joan were an absolute delight. Charlie was a joy to play music with as well, so when we both discovered that I couldn't keep up with him playing his version of *Tequila* he removed it from his set! It was an evening I'll never forget.

So rather late in my pro-am career as a rock drummer I had achieved my musical ambition to play with an internationally known star. For anyone who'd like to see more, videos are available on both my Facebook page and YouTube channel. There are also videos of my interviews with Charlie Gracie in 2019 while he was appearing with Marty Wilde in the Solid Gold Rock n Roll show. 2014 was also the year in which I successfully persuaded Mapex to give me a drum endorsement and my Meridian kit features prominently in most of my videos.

With the success of 2014. I decided to repeat the evening in 2015. However, it wasn't to be. Although Charlie Gracie did return along with Graham Fenton (ex-Matchbox), backed by Cornwall's Sugar Bullets and No Apologies. Unfortunately, I wasn't able to perform due to a brief unscheduled stay in Hospital. More importantly, and very sadly, neither was Ron Barrett who passed away in early 2015. During our rehearsals Ron used to say that he would die happy, if he never played guitar again, having performed with Charlie Gracie. Tragically, that was exactly what happened!

2016 dawned with an invitation to me, from the organisers of Cornwall's, '50s Mayhem Madness to perform with a band at their Rock 'n' Roll weekend! I then contacted Al Rideout and with KC Johnson put together the Guy Mackenzie Trio. In retrospect this was the best line-up I'd ever played with, especially as we concentrated on R 'n' R numbers which was a new venture for Al and KC (videos of The Guy Mackenzie Trio appear on both YouTube and Facebook)!

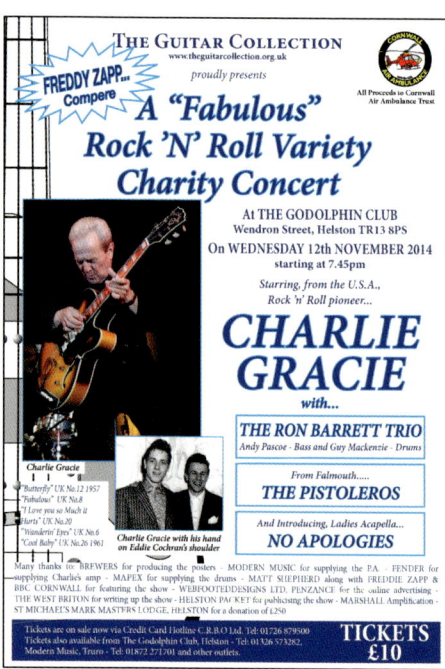

It was also my swan song. Since then I've only occasionally appeared on stage including once at Toni Carver's acoustic 'Cauldron' Sessions during the St Ives Festival in 2022 at the Western Hotel in St Ives.

Guy (back) providing percussion for singer/songwriter Kevin Sutcliffe, on harmonica, and vocalist Claire Young at the St Ives September Festival in 2022. Where he played with a reduced drum kit (pictured right) . *Photographs: James Ryall*

Chapter 22
The Guitar Collection
2005 – 2022

OVER THE YEARS and thanks to Ebay, I bought many guitars in the UK and Europe and also (especially in the "good old days" when the £1 = $2) quite a few from the USA. These included two Alamo guitars which had been built by a small manufacturer in the early '60s based in Texas. My kind hearted brother, Allan, also looked round the San Diego music shops and bought three for me.

I also own several instruments with links to well known bands and players including: a 1968 Hagstrom H8 bass which was believed to have once been owned by Phil Lynott of Thin Lizzie; A 1959 Burns Weill bass, originally owned by John Godfrey of Munro Jerry; A Guyatone LG50, a first guitar for British musicians such as: Marty Wilde, Hank Marvin and Jeff Beck. Not forgetting a Kurt Cobain "signature" Fender Jag-Stang and an Epiphone E270 as played by him in the *In Bloom* video and *Bleached Years*. Also, an Egmond Solid 7 dating from c.1963 and similar to Paul McCartney's first guitar which he played upside down as he was left handed!

Guy with part of his guitar collection pictured in 2008

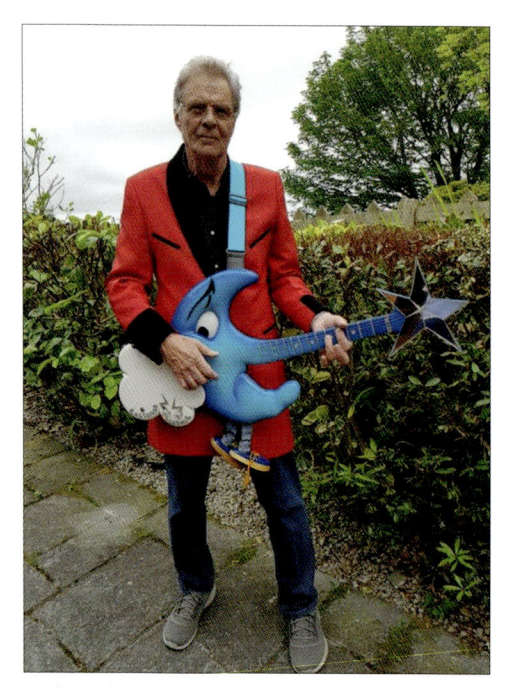

Guy, dressed in a Showaddywaddy drape jacket supplied by Andy George with the *Blue Moon* guitar and (right) admired by guitarist Phil Walker in 2019 amid the collection

Guy first reunited Showaddywaddy with the *Blue Moon* guitar in Falmouth during the band's 2010 UK tour

Thanks to Paul Day and some research, I managed to acquire the very first commercially built British solid electric guitars, the Supersounds which date from mid 1958! And, not just one but twelve, in various states of completeness too! Some real pieces of British musical history! But where did I discover them? In the basement of a house in Cheltenham!

Ever since I first bought a copy of the *Ultimate Guitar Book*, I'd lusted after the fabulous *Blue Moon* guitar which had been custom built for UK band Showaddywaddy to promote their cover version of that wonderful oldie *Blue Moon* which was released in 1980. The single charted early so British guitar maker, Brian Eastwood, worked flat-out for a sleepless 72 hours and it was delivered to the BBC TV's *Top of the Pops*' Studio with the paint drying!

But, who owned it now? Paul Day, of course, who had bought it in the 1980s. The band had ceased to use it partly because the then lead guitarist, Russell Field, found its dangling legs hanging, somewhat uncomfortably, below his midriff!

Paul sent it for auction but, when it didn't sell, I turned up on his doorstep with carrier bags full of used notes. I managed to buy it and it's been my guitar collection's "signature" guitar ever since. Soon after, in 2010, I reunited the band with the guitar and then in 2019 filmed them playing *Blue Moon* live on stage when their tour reached Redruth!

I have several favourite guitars and they include: a rare 80s Gibson Victory (so called as it was launched as a challenger to the Fender Stratocaster!), and a Fender Katana. This model was marketed to compete with the Jackson as played by Randy Rhodes, Ozzy Osborne's guitarist in the 1980s. Both were commercially unsuccessful and lasted for about 3 years. In a way, that's why I love them.

My 1980's Burns Bison which was the last guitar essentially hand-built by Jim Burns is also well loved. Not forgetting my Burns Mirage, probably the last of only about 20 built before Burns UK folded in 1978. I bought this on Ebay from Terry Dobson, guitarist of the band Black Lace – remember *Agadoo*. A few seconds before the end of the auction, I put in a "sniping" bid of what I thought was £351.99. However, the auction ended just seconds afterwards (it was too late to change my bid!) and I realised that I'd left out the decimal point – so my final bid was £35,199! Help! Luckily the price only reached £435 and I bought it. Over the years, I've had several offers, including one fairly recently from a wealthy collector in the USA, of $7,500 (then just over £5,000 but now thanks to the awful Liz "the lettuce" Truss – nearer to £7,000). It was cash upfront and sight unseen too but I still refused as, after all, where would I find another? Finally, my fabulously restored 1970s Burns Flyte which is identical to the guitar played by Lita Ford in The Runaways and also by Dave Hill of Slade and Marc Bolan.

Did I say that I can't play guitar? Well the secret's out, I can't! But I love them for their looks their style and the part they played in the history of Rock 'n' Roll and the development of popular music. Some people buy paintings and can't paint, I just buy electric guitars! But, as I can't play I get huge enjoyment from watching top musicians playing my instruments and appearing in my videos such as Phil Walker of *The Story of Guitar Heroes*, rising star, Kris Barras and Cornwall's (maybe the UKs?) no. 1 bass player. David Greenaway. As a result of my website I've also met, interviewed and become friends with several well known musicians, including stars such as fellow guitar collector, Frank Allen of The Searchers, drummer Barry Whitwam of Herman's Hermits (who's still into *Something Good* after 58 years!), TV Smith of The Adverts and, British legend, Marty Wilde MBE.

My guitars have been featured in several books including seventy in *1001 Guitars*, sixteen in *The Complete Illustrated Book of the Electric Guitar* and of course *The Ultimate Guitar Book*. I've appeared on BBC TV's *Antiques Roadshow* BBC TV's *Antiques Road Trip* and, with my Supersound guitars, on BBC TV's *South West* – well I did find them in Cheltenham!

In case you'd like to know, I currently own over 200 instruments and my Collection is still growing. Also. if you type "The Guitar Collection" into your Google search engine, you'll find my collection still at the top of about 200 million results!

Sally with bass guitarist Roger Newell, a founding member of the English Rock Ensemble who Guy interviewed for his YouTube channel, The Guitar Collection, in 2016. Roger, who played with Rick Wakeman and Marty Wilde and The Wildcats sadly died in September 2021

Chapter 23
Glenmuick
1948 – 2022

MY FATHER SOLD Glenmuick Estate, to Sir Ian Walker-Okeover Bt. in 1948. The sale included our family burial ground, crypt and St Nathalan's chapel which was built by my great grandfather James Thompson Mackenzie. However, in the early '60s, my father heard that the chapel was to be demolished and I remember how upset he was when this news reached him. When all seemed lost, he asked The Royal Family for their help in saving our family chapel. Sadly the main building didn't survive but, thanks to the intervention of the Queen Mother, it's tower still remains today! The beautiful altar, various other items including the Mackenzie panel window and a Register of Baptisms, were then gifted to St Kentigern's church in Ballater and they are still there now. In 1967 my father gifted St Kentigern's a gilt chalice and paten in a wooden case, "not to be removed without his or his heirs permission", they also remain there. And, I have one of the two family Bibles.

In the early 2000s, thanks to the Walker-Okeover family and, more recently, the present Baronet, Sir Andrew Walker-Okeover, the Mackenzie family now have a long secure, repairing lease over our family burial ground, crypt and tower. Over the years, we have stabilised the tower, cut down and removed a number of trees which had passed their "sell by" date. However, the storms of early 2022 caught us out! Two very large trees were blown over in the area of the crypt (hopefully not damaging the structure) and they are still to be removed. The falling trees also demolished a part of the wall surrounding it which I had reconstructed in 2019 at great expense!

About 10 or so years ago I met Alistair Cassie, Chairman of the Ballater Local History Group for the first time. Later, in 2017, he was awarded the BEM for community work in and around Ballater!

The surviving tower of St Nathalan's chapel which was built by Guy's great grandfather James Thompson Mackenzie

But, then, he had another project on the go although I wasn't initially certain what it was! However, as time went on, I realised that Alistair was organising teams of volunteers to restore the Come & Rest Memorial Seat overlooking Ballater which had been built in memory of my Grandfather, Allan Russell Mackenzie 2nd Bt. following his death in 1906 "by his many friends" at their own expense! Since then, it had fallen into disrepair

In due course I, along with family members, was invited by Alistair to a 'Special Day' on Sunday 1st November 2015. Of course I asked Alistair what was going to happen but his reply was: "Och it's a wee celebration, nothing to worry about!"

The day dawned and, with my sister Lucy, who had come from the Isle of Mull and my brother, Allan, who had flown in from his home in California, we left our hotel and drove over the Royal Bridge in Ballater and parked our cars at the appointed time. We then started walking up the path to the Memorial but no sooner had we started than we became aware of two bagpipers following us playing their pipes! We suddenly realised that they were piping the Mackenzies up to the Come & Rest Memorial! It's hard to describe how emotional it was for each of us to be piped back onto what had once been our family Estate – Glenmuick

When we reached the Memorial, there was a considerable crowd present which included the volunteers, local people and onlookers! The Come & Rest Memorial seat had been painstakingly restored with every attention to detail. It looked amazing – surely as good as it must have done over 100 years previously when it was first built! It was an absolute credit to the hard work and dedication, over several years, of everyone who had contributed to a quite remarkable transformation which will surely last for another 100 years!

We then found ourselves the centre of attention and toasts (whisky, of course!) were drunk. Thankfully the official video doesn't include everything I said in reply to Alistair Cassie's speech. As I concluded my thanks, with the welcome we'd received, I was simply overwhelmed and, as a result, my emotions just got the better of me! I'd always realised that our family had been held in high regard in the area, but I didn't realise until that day just how much the Mackenzie family had meant to the townsfolk of Ballater and seemingly still does!

As Alistair Cassie said, it really was a 'Special Day' and one that Allan, Lucy and I will never forget!

The beautiful War Memorial at Ballater

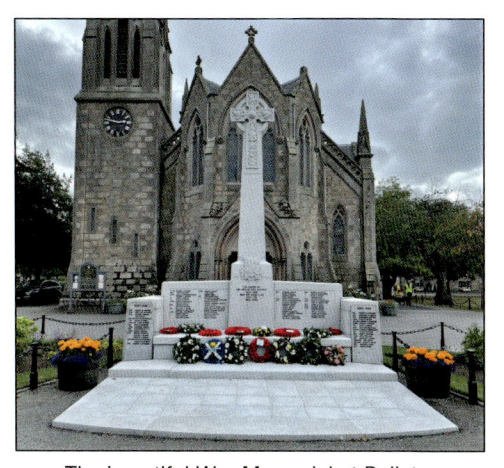

Sally walking to lay the wreath at the War Memorial

2022 was the year that local historian, John Burrows, completed his book *The Ballater Memorial: Does it Make You Remember?* which, remarkably, contained details of almost everyone whose names were inscribed on the Ballater War Memorial! This included, of course, my late uncle Allan Keith "Sloper" Mackenzie who had been killed at the Somme in 1916. John Burrows also organised a Re-dedication of the Monument Service on Sunday 24th July. Sally along with my stepson Trevor (who also acted as her co-driver!) attended as did Amanda, my granddaughter Scarlet and my son-in-law Ian. My cousin (my mother's brother, Billy Innes' son) Jonathan with his wife Jane also attended.

It was another remarkable day with a Lone Piper playing *Flowers of the Forest* and addresses including from Ed Farquharson who represented the Lord Lieutenant of Aberdeenshire, and Clan Farquharson. Sally laid the wreath on behalf of our family and the Ballater Pipe band commenced and closed the ceremony. They played everyone from the Victoria Hall and, afterwards, back again for tea and light refreshments. As Ian wrote later: "It was a privilege to be part of the Special Day" and Trevor keeps saying: "We must go back to Scotland"!

Finally I must mention David Morrison as mine, and the Mackenzie family's debt of gratitude to him is heartfelt. He worked for Glenmuick Estate all his life and has looked after our family burial ground almost since my father sold up. He still undertakes this duty today!

> **Postscript**: My Uncle Billy was a truly remarkable man who bravely survived four years as a Japanese prisoner of war working on the Burma railway! Sometime after the sad, untimely, death of my aunt Alison he married Patricia at the age of 90. Then, shortly before his death aged 93 Uncle Billy was granted the Freedom of the City of Aberdeen!

The Mackenzie family at Ballater from (l to r): Jonathan Innes, granddaughter Scarlet, Amanda, son-in-law Ian, stepson Trevor and Sally

The Mackenzie of Glenmuick plaque at the Come & Rest Memorial Seat

Chapter 24
Epilogue
2022

IT NEVER OCCURRED to me that I'd ever write a book, let alone one about my own life! However, lock-downs came and with a minor amount of prompting from my future son-in-law Rob, Iona's fiancée, about my life in London, I was off. But, when the seriousness of the pandemic ceased and life started to return to 'a new' normal! so did my workload, consequently I never had time to complete my life story. The book had, more or less, ended in 1990 when I was aged 44. However, with some (actually quite a lot!) of prompting by my editor and publisher, Toni Carver, I endeavoured to bring my 'memories' up to date. Chapters (actually quite a few!) were added and here are a few final thoughts and memories.

Family Life

Once Amanda had a taste of London with Martin Kennedy-Bell, she moved there soon afterwards with her friend Jessica. They had some savings when they left but no job or home, however, within 24 hours, they had both. Amanda's been in London ever since and she now leads an international life-style as personal assistant to a businessman with homes, literally, all over the world.

Some years afterwards I remember seeing Iona, in her first job, behind the counter of the Bradford & Bingley Building Society in Redruth. Imagine my surprise when, just a few days later (it seemed) she also relocated to London where she has worked her way up in the world of media and is now employed by ITV as an executive producer. Of course, we see them on high days and holidays and I occasionally make the trek to London but hate to leave Cornwall.

Two "treks" involved seeing The Pirates at the Half Moon in Putney in the early 2000s. The Pirates were British Rock 'n' Roll star Johnny Kidd's backing band prior to his untimely death in 1966 and this line-up later became a high energy pub rock band. Of course the band loved being photographed with Amanda and Iona and I was able to chat again with one of my guitar heroes, Mick Green. Mick always teased me, whenever I saw him, by saying: "What do you need all those guitars for, you only need one!" And, he did only need one!

In Cornwall in 2007 my friend, fellow guitar collector, acclaimed author and bass player of The Searchers (since 1964!) Frank Allen called round to my home to talk guitars. Amanda and 7 month old Scarlet, who just happened to be in Cornwall then, joined us and Frank, who has no children of his own (I don't think so anyway—mindful of the "willy fiddling incident" with Dusty Springfield which he recounts in *The Searchers and Me*!) was quite delightful with Scarlet and I photographed him giving Scarlet her very first guitar lesson! She's never looked back and plays guitar (and drums) today!

My birthday present from Iona in 2014 was an overnight stay in a hotel overlooking Loch Lomond and from there we went on to the Isle of Mull to stay with Lucy. My birthday coincided with my preparation (rehearsals, ticket sales etc.) for the Charlie Gracie Concert and I arrived in Glasgow with a bad cold and slightly wishing that the date could have been altered. But, the hotel was fabulous and after a dinner of haggis and chips (I'd eaten haggis and I'd eaten chips but never together) washed down with a few malt whiskies we both, unsurprisingly, slept well. The next day after a walk down to the "bonny banks" of the loch, my cold had gone so we had a wonderful holiday.

It is always a pleasure seeing Trevor, (when he's here he's usually working on updating and helping me with my computer! Where would I be without his expertise, I ask myself?) at his home in Torquay, with his family. Gabriel never fails to say when I come to their house "grandfather, let me show you my room!" And, for me it's so unusual to visit a house which has a real folly (a gazebo?) in the garden!

Follies & Unusual Buildings

Apart from music, my love of follies and unusual buildings were effectively the only positives of my time at Stowe. And, what I previously had omitted to write about was that I once tried to buy a folly! Not just any folly but a huge 100 foot tower. Towards the end of 1971, just after I bought my first flat, Martin Bellamy rang me to say that there was a small ruinous tower called Guy's Folly near where he lived in Gloucestershire. It was up for sale.

I had no idea of the price, neither did Martin, but I drove up to look at it. Then – a double whammy, not only was it sold but also scheduled for demolition to be replaced by a telecommunication mast! Somewhat downcast, on my way back to London, I was driving through Faringdon, when I noticed a huge tower on the hill just outside the town. Of course, I had to have a closer look and what I saw was a forlorn looking building, apparently forgotten and with its doorway and lower windows bricked-up. With a nothing ventured, nothing gained attitude (yep, that's me!), I asked around and located the owner, Robert Herbert-Percy who owned Faringdon House and Estate which he'd inherited following the death of his much older "companion" the eccentric composer and novelist Gerald Hugh Tyrwhitt-Wilson, 14th Baron Berners. Umm, now didn't he once invite a horse to dinner?!

I contacted Robert about the possibility of him selling me Faringdon Tower although goodness knows how I might have paid for it! He invited me to lunch at Faringdon House to discuss it after he had organised his Estate workers to show me the inside via a very long ladder. After some thought, he told me that he wouldn't sell it as it had been built for him as a 21st birthday present by Lord Berners but he would be prepared to lease it to me on a 21 year repairing lease at a cost of £50 a year. Consequently, via a friend in Lloyds, I found a Chartered

Surveyor who for just £2 an hour (cash!) agreed to survey it for me. His advice was effectively: "Do not touch it with a barge-pole" as it needed completely repointing so, sadly, my interest ended here.

I've never owned a folly except the little one I now have on my land in Cornwall which I call "Solomon's Tower" after my friend Paul Solomon who built it – or "Guy's Folly" – so I have had to be content with visiting many.

When I first heard of Painshill in Surrey, with its gardens a "shambles" and its buildings in "ruins" (*Monumental Follies* by Stuart Barton) I never expected to see the wonderful transformation and return to what was once described as "one of the finest and most beautifully landscaped gardens in the country" which it is today! The grotto is simply magnificent and, on the day I went there, I hoped to climb the tower but, sadly, that wasn't to be as the guide assigned to that function had decided to take the day off!

Stourhead, in particular, Alfred's Tower is definitely "up there" among my favourites, especially as it is 161 feet high! And, yes, I've been to the top (how could I possible resist!) and what a view there is from there!

In life you don't have to be big to be beautiful or, for that matter, interesting. The same is true with follies! And, that's the case with The Knill Monument in Cornwall! Built by a customs officer and former mayor of St Ives in 1782 and evidently determined that his name should live on John Knill made provision in his will that every 5 years on July 25th, ten virgins and two women, the widows of fishermen or miners should be employed to dance round the pyramid singing the Hundredth Psalm! That tradition still carries on! John Knill intended the Monument to be his mausoleum – it has a small vault within – but unfortunately he was in London when he died so is interred in St Andrew's Church, Holborn.

During the 1980s I happened to be driving past the magical Hadlow Castle (May's Folly) in Kent. There was a team of builders undertaking restoration work on the building on that day and I couldn't resist asking if I could go inside. They very kindly agreed. However I spent so much time inside and, especially at the top, that I was met with some very puzzled looks when I returned to earth! Maybe they thought that in some way, I had joined the original builder who was, I believe, buried at the top!

There are so many others I could mention or write another book about if I could have ever found time! However, I must include Clavell Tower at Kimmeridge in Dorset. Sited on the edge of the cliff, when I first saw it, it was in a ruinous state which allowed me to explore the inside! Now, many years later, not only has it been beautifully restored but has also been moved 25 metres inland as, with coastal erosion in its previous location, it would probably have toppled over by now!

Finally, nobody who visits Oban, can possibly forget McCaig's folly which is a huge Colosseum built above the town by a wealthy banker to provide work for the men of the district in times of hardship. Most notable for me was that it was almost the first building I saw in the town when coming into Oban by boat from

Mull. It was, however, never completed and some people said John McCaig, unsurprisingly, ran out of money before he "put the roof on" but he certainly died before it was completed!

VIPs – Very Important Pets

In our lives there have been some very important pets. For my birthday in 1990, Sally gave me a huge box which seemed empty! I was a bit surprised at this and started to rattle it – much to Sally's alarm as it contained a tiny black and white kitten who I soon named, Mittens! A few years later, he actually saved our lives when, one cold night with all our windows tightly closed, our Rayburn's chimney somehow got blocked sending carbon monoxide fumes into our house. Mittens must have had a fit as he screamed, waking us up! Sadly, Sally's old cat, Bella, was overcome but everyone else survived with no lasting ill effects. We were so fortunate not to have been 2 of the 40 or so people who die of carbon monoxide poisoning in the UK each year – thanks to our VIP! Mittens was very much my cat and lived to the age of 15 despite being challenged for his position as top cat by my mother's part Burmese cat, Taurus, who came to live with us with her in 1995. In his way, Mittens was my best friend, and I still miss him.

After Bruno died we got a German Shepherd who we called Gerry and, after Gemma died, a border collie, we called Bonnie. Both were very adept at doing disappearing acts and Bonnie once ended up at a farm about 2 miles away – thank goodness we knew the farmer who kept her until we went to get her back, armed with a bottle of wine as a thank you! So, in an effort to give both dogs something to focus on, I started taking them out with me in the back of my Citroen Xantia.

In those days I was chief maintenance man (and rent collector before the days of direct debits) for our rental properties so I was out most days armed to the teeth with silicone, 6" nails, gaffer tape and an assortment of tools! Consequently the dogs always waited patiently for me to drive out and reminded me not to forget them! When my working day ended, they knew we'd go for a walk – the more remote the better, as they could run loose, at places such as Chun Quoit, Carn Kenidjack and the Men-an-Tol, all on the moors in West Cornwall. These were favourites along with the coast path, beaches such as Hayle with its 3 miles of golden sands and Long Rock near Penzance.

In 2007 Sally got a black pug puppy who she called Porgy. As soon as we saw him, we both fell in love with him, he was the dearest little dog. Later we found out he was also the bravest. Sadly, from the first week with us, we found that he had health issues. In due course our vet and friend, Luke Stevens, successfully carried out a major operation on him when he was less than a year old. But, at just 18 months old, he was found to have a liver shunt which allowed blood to shunt or bypass the liver. He very sadly died following an operation in Bristol.

Following Porgy's death, Sally got Lottie, a fawn pug. Lottie proved to be the start of a successful dog showing career for Sally. At one time we had eleven pugs. Sally travelled all over the UK winning lots of awards, including at Crufts on

CH POPINJAY PHILHARMONIC OF SUPERSOUND JW
Wil
DOB 16/5/17
5 CCs & 5 Res CCs

Sally Lady Mackenzie - Cornwall
Photos by Alan V Walker

several occasions, UK Champion Pug and winning Top Dog of Cornwall! I have to admit, that the huge number of pugs which we owned was partly down to me. Over time, four which we were asked to re-home, stayed with us as I simply didn't want to let them go!

The smallest pug of all, Rosie, insisted on coming on all my walks with Bess our French bulldog, after Gerry and Bonnie had both died. Rosie, now aged almost 15, was, and still is a real trooper. She only asked to be picked up if the water in the footpaths on the moors reached her chin! But, she did always wear a waterproof coat when it rained!

In 1990s Sally achieved an ambition of having a farming enterprise. She had 2 milking cows and several droves of pigs which she bought as piglets, selling them on later after they'd been butchered. Of course, with their part milk diet, the pork was evidently delicious and so we had no problem selling it locally, although I couldn't bring myself to eat an animal which had been raised here!

Following Wooky's death, Sally's most important horse was "D" (for Demelza) who lived to be 33 and is still here – buried in her favourite field next to our house!

For the future we have eight fawn pugs: (Brian) Ferry a German Shepherd puppy and Tim a black pug with one eye who I couldn't let go after we'd been asked to re-home him. Tim is very lazy but a real character who decided to feature in my video of the John Bailey guitar being played live by our neighbour, Pat! What a star!

Exploring Cornwall, Devon and Dorset

Ever since my mother first took me exploring on Mull, exploring has been one of my most important hobbies. I can never entirely understand why anyone would want to go abroad – apart that is for a change of scenery or a warmer climate – as there are so many wonderful places to visit in the UK.

I have so much enjoyed exploring Cornwall, Devon and beyond: by car, train (steam sometimes) and on foot. However, I'll start with the Derbyshire Peak District which I visited in about 1969 with my then companion "Miss Piggy". I just had to visit the Blue John Cavern, along with others, having read and enjoyed *The Terror of Blue John Gap* by Sir Arthur Conan Doyle (by chance I have a letter written by him to Rosita Forbes, my cousin Pam's mother). What a fantastic atmosphere the cave has and, of course, I had to buy a very small piece of Blue John on my very small budget. After visiting the cavern it was easy to see how Conan Doyle could write the story he did!

Cornwall has such a wide variety of wonderful places, it's hard to know what to include here. Perhaps a good place to start is at the end so now to Porthgwarra which is a small cove near Land's End. Interestingly it has two tunnels built through the rocks. The first so that seaweed could be collected from the beach to use as a fertiliser and the second leading to shellfish storage areas. Walking from there towards Land's End, and I usually had my dogs with me on nearly all my walks, firstly my dear Bruno and a rescue Rottweiler called Gemma (who always walked behind me, while Bruno ran in front!) to Carn Les Boel, a huge oval stone which was the start of the St Michael energy line. And, the first time I visited, I decided to walk a little further and discovered the magical Nanjizal, which at that time I'd never heard of! Nanjizal is a sandy cove with a remarkable rock arch in front of which is a magical tidal pool. Don't miss it if you're anywhere near, its simply unforgettable!

I've walked most of the Cornwall parts of the South West coast path but only in sections – unlike, for example, Raynor Winn the author of *The Salt Path* who undertook the whole walk penniless, after becoming homeless. The section between Porthcurno and the Logan Rock is probably one of the most photographed sections of coastline in the UK. Between those two locations is Pedn Vounder beach which is possibly one of the most beautiful beaches in the world especially as it's tucked away at the bottom of steep cliffs. It's like being in a different world which, of course it is, especially with it's relaxed attitude to clothing! It was one of Sally and my favourite beaches (Oh no! we're not telling, you'll have to make your own mind up!) There are 3 ways to get down the cliff. The first was "don't look down!" difficult. The second was known as the Goat Path and even more precarious. The third was for experienced rock climbers only as it was seemingly vertical for the first section anyway. As well as being a "nudist beach" the granite cliffs make it a popular "bouldering" venue for rock climbers. I still remember lying underneath this part with Sally while an experienced lady climber decided to climb up, literally above where I was lying sunbathing. And, she had taken full advantage of the beach's "no clothing" option too!

While still in West Cornwall, I must mention Boscawen-un, a stone circle, where Sally saw a ghost! Sally and I had heard about this stone circle in the 1990s and decided to try and seek it out. As things transpired we had some difficulty discovering it but when we did, we found it remarkably atmospheric and well hidden. There was another person in the circle when we arrived and it almost seemed if he was guarding it as he certainly didn't appear friendly – of course he may have been in the middle of some pagan ritual which we'd interrupted! Anyway, we decided to come back on the following day. As luck would have it, Sally by chance had tried to shut the back door of our Peugeot 305 van before I'd got my head out of the way, so we had something of a row! Consequently Sally decided that she wouldn't come all the way to the circle and sat down on an outcrop of rock overlooking it while I went on my own. Thankfully, this time there was no one in the circle so I was able to appreciate it on my own. I then walked back to the car collecting Sally on the way. When we got to the car Sally said to me: "What did that man say to you?" I replied: "What man?". She then said: "the man who followed you round the circle," I replied: "There was nobody there"!

I've always loved steam trains and have been on all the steam railways in Cornwall and Devon. My favourite is the train which travels from Paignton, along the spectacular English Riviera coast, then through Long Wood and along the Dart Estuary to Kingswear—just over the estuary from Dartmouth. However my number one small railway is the Looe Valley railway which runs from Liskeard to Looe then when it leaves Liskeard station, has to reverse before descending a sharp incline into the valley of the river Looe. On the day I travelled on it, I had decided to alight at St Keyne Wishing Well halt and then catch the next train at Causeland. However, as soon as I got on the train, Amanda rang me. She was very upset and I talked to her for most of the journey to St. Keyne in an effort to cheer her up. I then alighted and walked up the hill to the Wishing Well where I made a wish for her and threw in some coins as was the custom. It must have been successful as I didn't hear from her again for several days and she seemed to have completely recovered when I did!

North Devon is more remote than one would expect but it also has some magical places to visit. My favourite cliff railway is the amazing water powered and very steep, funicular which was built in 1890 and joins the towns of Lynton and Lynmouth. Well worth a trip, fabulous views but don't look down if you stand at the front!

Not far away is Ilfracombe with its Victorian tunnels through the cliffs to the sea water bathing pools which, when built in the 1800s were segregated! Evidently, men swam naked but women had to cover up!

Not forgetting, Woody Bay with its forlorn remains of one man's ambition to create another Lynton/Lynmouth with cliff railway and bathing pools. Sadly the enterprise ended in bankruptcy in 1900 and a prison sentence for Col. Benjamin

Lake whose dream it had all been! But, for me, it was still worth the mile long walk to see the remains of the pier and the bathing pool and visualise that dream!

With the advent of "lock down" in 2020 Sally had achieved her every ambition in the world of dog shows so she stopped showing pugs. She now has become a devoted gardener who is currently transforming a field with ponds, a stone circle, raised beds and also a kitchen garden which in mid-November 2022, was still producing vegetables!

For the Future

As for my future plans; top of the list is a visit to the house Iona and Rob have just bought in Twickenham.

Then, I'd like to visit Tyneham, the lost village in Dorset as it was closed the last time I went there.

I must see The Searchers live on stage again on what will surely be their last tour, although they actually did "retire" in 2018! It will be great to catch up once more with: Frank Allen, Spencer James, John McNally and meet the new boy, Richie Burns.

Maybe one more gig, the '50's Mayhem Madness R&R weekend next May perhaps?

And, of course, visit Glenmuick after the fallen trees have been removed from the crypt and supervise (pay for!) the necessary restoration work!

Also, there is a long overdue live interview with Alan Lovell of the Swinging Blue Jeans and why not another with new, Cornwall based singing star, Gilly Lee-White who I helped promote for a while?

I have just heard there's a rare "must have" 1980's Burns Scorpion bass guitar in next month's Gardiner Houlgate guitar auction near Bath.

So the Party ain't over yet, oh no... The Party ain't over yet!

Appendix

As the reader will have gathered Guy Mackenzie has a considerable presence on the World Wide Web. For those interested in following up on aspects of Guy's memories and keeping up with his interests online here are the links

The Genealogy and Family Trees of Mackenzie of Glenmuick
https://www.mackenzie-glenmuick.org.uk

This website Includes:

The Innes of Balvenie

Foster-Forbes Family Connections

Innes of Raemoir

Forbes & Innes Family Tree.

Mackenzie Memorial Come & Rest Renovation Project:

http://mackenziememorial.weebly.com

Clan Mackenzie Society of Scotland and the UK

https://clanmackenziesociety.co.uk

May We Be Britons: A History of the Mackenzies by Andrew Mckenzie

http://www.historyofthemackenzies.co.uk

This website includes the Mackenzie Involvement at the Battle of Glenshiel in 1719. A Talk by Andrew Mckenzie.

The Guitar Collection of Guy Mackenzie
https://www.theguitarcollection.org.uk

This website features collection of old, rare and unusual electric guitars

The Guitar Collection YouTube Channel
https://www.youtube.com/user/GuitarCollectionUK

The Guitar Collection Facebook Page
https://www.facebook.com/guysguitarcollection

Other interesting website linked to The Guitar Collection

The Supersound Story. The UK's first "commercially built" solid electric guitars:
https://www.supersound.org.uk

Supersound Electronic Products on Wikipedia
https://en.wikipedia.org/wiki/Supersound_Electronic_Products

Family Websites

Allan Mackenzie. Hands On Real Estate Experts
http://marventures.com

Lucy Mackenzie: Lip Na Cloiche Garden and Nursery on the Isle of Mull
https://www.lipnacloiche.co.uk

Vittoria Panizzon: A World Class Equestrian who has represented Italy at Three Olympic Games
https://www.vittoriapanizzon.com

Guy's Historic Property Websites

The Wheal Buller Project. An Illustrated Account of its History and Preservation
https://www.whealbullerproject.co.uk

The Count House, Ding Dong Mine and its Association with Richard Trevithick:
https://www.dingdongcounthouse.org.uk

Guy's Speeches Website

Farewell Speech as a District Councillor and 2 others
https://www.theguitarcollection.org.uk/speeches

Also

Guy's Instagram Page. Places and Music
https://www.instagram.com/mackenzie.guy

Guy's Personal Facebook Page
https://www.facebook.com/guy.mackenzie.79